I0113339

RWANDA 1994

RWANDA 1994: GENOCIDE IN THE "LAND OF A THOUSAND HILLS"

Benyamin Neuberger

equinox

SHEFFIELD UK   BRISTOL CT

Published by Equinox Publishing Ltd.

UK: Office 415, The Workstation, 15 Paternoster Row, Sheffield, South Yorkshire S1 2BX

USA: ISD, 70 Enterprise Drive, Bristol, CT 06010

www.equinoxpub.com

First published in Hebrew by the Open University of Israel, Raanana, 2005. This English, updated edition published in 2017 by Equinox Publishing Ltd

© Benyamin Neuberger 2017
Translated from the Hebrew by Geremy Forman.

All rights reserved. No part of this publication may be reproduced or transmitted in any form or by any means, electronic or mechanical, including photocopying, recording or any information storage or retrieval system, without prior permission in writing from the publishers.

British Library Cataloguing-in-Publication Data
A catalogue record for this book is available from the British Library.
ISBN-13   978-1-78179-579-8 (hardback)
978-1-78179-580-4 (paperback)

Library of Congress Cataloging-in-Publication Data
Neuberger, Ralph Benyamin, 1943–
Rwanda 1994 : genocide in the "Land of a thousand hills" / by Benyamin Neuberger.
G'enosaid. English | Genocide in the "Land of a Thousand Hills"
English, updated edition. | Bristol, CT : Equinox Publishing Ltd, 2017. | "First published in Hebrew by the Open University of Israel, Raanana, 2005. This English, updated edition published in 2017 by Equinox Publishing Ltd." | Includes biblio-graphical references and index.
LCCN 2017000046 (print) | LCCN 2017000640 (ebook) | ISBN 9781781795798 (hb) | ISBN 9781781795804 (pb) | ISBN 9781781795811 (ePDF)
Subjects: LCSH: Rwanda—History—Civil War, 1994—Atrocities. | Genocide—Rwanda. | Rwanda—Ethnic relations. | Tutsi (African people)—Crimes against—Rwanda—History—20th century. | Hutu (African people)—Rwanda—Politics and government—20th century. | Genocide.
LCC DT450.435 .N3813 2017 (print) | LCC DT450.435 (ebook) | DDC 967.5710431--dc23 LC record available at https://lccn.loc.gov/2017000046

Typeset by CAUFIELD COPYEDITING AND TYPESETTING

Printed and bound in Great Britain by Lightning Source Inc. (La Vergne, TN), Lightning Source UK Ltd.

Contents

List of Figures

List of Tables

List of Maps

List of Illustrations

Abbreviations

ADEP-Mizero	*Alliance pour la démocratie, l'équité et le progrès* (Alliance for Democracy, Equity and Progress)
AFDL	*Alliance des forces démocratiques pour la libération du Congo-Zaïre* (Alliance of Democratic Forces for the Liberation of Congo-Zaire)
ALR	*Armée pour la libération du Rwanda* (Army for the Liberation of Rwanda)
APC	Armored Personnel Carrier
APROSOMA	*Association pour la promotion sociale des masses* (Association for the Social Advancement of the Masses)
BBTG	Broad-Based Transitional Government
CDR	*Coalition pour la défense de la république* (Coalition for the Defense of the Republic)
DRC	Democratic Republic of Congo
FAR	*Force armée rwandaise* (Rwandan Armed Forces; see also RGF)
FDD	*Forces pour la défense de la démocratie* (Forces for the Defense of Democracy)
FNL	*Forces nationales de libération* (National Forces for Liberation)
FRODEBU	*Front pour la démocratie au Burundi* (Front for Democracy in Burundi)
FRONASA	Front for National Salvation
ICTR	International Criminal Tribunal for Rwanda

JDR	*Jeunesse démocrate républicaine* (Democratic Republican Youth)
LIPRODHOR	*Ligue pour la promotion et la défense des droits de l'homme au Rwanda* (Rwandan League for the Promotion and Defense of Human Rights)
MDR	*Mouvement démocratique républicain* (Democratic Republican Movement)
MDR-PARMEHUTU	*Mouvement démocratique républicain—Parti du mouvement de l'émancipation Hutu* (Democratic Republican Movement—Party of the Hutu Emancipation Movement)
MRND	*Mouvement révolutionaire national pour le développement* (National Revolutionary Movement for Development)
MRNDD	*Mouvement républicain national pour la démocratie et le développement* (National Republican Mouvement for Democracy and Development)
MSF	*Médecins sans frontières* (Doctors without Borders)
MSM	*Mouvement social Muhutu* (Hutu Social Movement)
NRA	National Resistance Army
OAU	Organization of African Unity
OIF	*Organisation internationale de la francophonie* (International Organization of the French-speaking World)
PARMEHUTU	*Parti du mouvement de l'émancipation des Bahutu* (Party of the Movement for the Emancipation of the Bahutu)

PDC	*Parti démocratique chrétien* (Christian Democratic Party)
PDR	*Parti démocratique de renouveau* (Democratic Party for Renewal)
PL	*Parti libéral* (Liberal Party)
PSD	*Parti social démocrate* (Social Democratic Party)
RADER	*Rassemblement démocratique rwandais* (Democratic Assembly of Rwanda)
RGF	Rwandan Government Forces (see also FAR)
RPF	Rwandan Patriotic Front
RTLMC	*Radio télévision libre des Mille Collines* (Free Radio Television of a Thousand Hills)
SAP	Structural Adjustment Program
UNAMIR	United Nations Assistance Mission to Rwanda
UNAR	*Union nationale rwandaise* (Rwandan National Union)
UPRONA	*Union pour le progrès national* (Union for National Progress)

Acknowledgements

I am deeply grateful to the Open University of Israel, which originally published the book in Hebrew, and to its president, Prof. Jacob (Kobi) Metzer, for transferring the copyrights to me. My deep appreciation to Dr. Catherine Caufield for a truly excellent editing job. Thanks also to Equinox Publishing for their support. And, of course, many thanks to my wife Belina for her help, love, and patience.

INTRODUCTION

In his introduction to the original Hebrew version of *Rwanda 1994: Genocide in the Land of a Thousand Hills*, Yair Auron, a well-known genocide scholar, writes that

> one aim of this book on the Rwandan genocide is to increase the sensitivity of students, scholars and other readers to the phenomenon of genocide. Another is to encourage them to . . . [reflect on their] responsibility vis-à-vis such acts of injustice and to consider possible ways of taking action to prevent them, whether as individuals or in conjunction with other members of their own ethnocultural or social group. The fundamental principle underlying this book is the universal value of human life.

I completely identify with these words, but would like to add a more personal note. The Holocaust, the genocide of the Jews between 1939 and 1945, has had a deep impact on my life. My wife is a holocaust survivor and many members of both our families were murdered by the Nazis. We grew up hoping that this would be the last time such barbaric events take place. "Never again" was a prevalent phrase often uttered at the time. Unfortunately, it remained only a phrase. What happened in Rwanda in 1994, a mere half century after World War II, was a call-up, warning all of us that it could happen again, and that it would do so unless we faced out responsibilities and actively opposed this evil. Leviticus 19:16 teaches "neither shalt thou stand aside when mischief befalls thy neighbour." These are the reasons why this book was written and why the genocide in Rwanda should be studied widely.

The term genocide, as well as its inclusion in international law, is of recent origin, although the praxis of killing entire populations certainly is not a new phenomenon. The origin of the word is from the Greek *genos* (descent, people, race) and the Latin *caedere* (slaughter, kill). It was coined during World War II by Raphael Lemkin, a Jewish-Polish lawyer and holocaust survivor, and the architect of the United Nations Convention on the Prevention and Punishment of the Crime of Genocide (1948). Article 2 of the convention defines genocide as [...] any of the following acts committed with intent to destroy in whole or in part a national, racial or religious group such as:

1. killing members of the group;

2. causing serious bodily or mental harm to members of the group;

3. deliberately inflicting on the group conditions of life calculated to bring about its physical destruction in whole or in part;

4. imposing measures intended to prevent births within the group;

5. forcibly transferring children of the group to another group.

This definition relates to intentional killing. Because of the USSR's Stalinist regime's opposition, it omits the mass killing of political and social groups, such as the bourgeoisie or the peasantry (all of the latter were accused of being rich kulaks, i.e. affluent landlords) in the USSR and the city dwellers in the Cambodian democide in the late 1970s. In order to expand this definition, another term, namely democide—i.e. the killing of the demos, or people—was coined. Today, the term genocide applies mainly to the killing of ethnonational groups. In the case of Rwanda, the term genocide is most apt since it refers to the killing of the Tutsi people, though the term democide is also relevant, since tens of thousands of Hutu who fiercely opposed the genocidal government were also murdered.

It is now more than two decades since the world stood by, idly witnessing the Rwandan genocide. During the one hundred days of killing nearly one million men, women and children were murdered. In many ways, the Rwandan genocide marked the victory of evil: not only were people murdered by their own countrymen, neighbors, friends, and religious leaders, but it was a genocide that had been foreseen and that could have been prevented.

This book explores the Rwandan genocide's historical background, the genocidal ideology and political context (its perpetrators and victims, and the strategy and 'methodology' of the killings); its international dimensions (in particular the involvement or calculated non-involvement of France, the US, Belgium, the UN and the other African countries); and the dire question of whether the world could have prevented the massacre. It further draws parallels between the Rwandan genocide and other genocides in the twentieth century; and relates to the policy of punishing the murderers by the International Criminal Tribunal for Rwanda in Arusha, Tanzania, and by the traditional judicial system called gacaca. Finally, it dwells briefly on what happened in Rwanda after the genocide.

1

HISTORICAL AND POLITICAL BACKGROUND

Let's exterminate them all!

(Des Forges 1999, 260)

Rwanda, a small country located in the heart of Africa, is widely known as the "Land of a Thousand Hills" or the "Land of Eternal Spring." Tragically, between April and July 1994, the country's majestic landscape served as the backdrop for one of the most brutal genocides the world has known since World War II, when some 800–900 thousand people were killed in only a few weeks. The great majority of the victims were Tutsi, while the rest were Hutu and Twa (according to estimates, the genocide took the lives of 800,000 of the 930,000 Tutsi living in Rwanda at the time).

Although some have opposed classifying these events as genocide,[1] there is no doubt that the Tutsi were murdered neither because of their actions or views, nor spontaneously in wartime; rather, their murders resulted from a carefully planned and unconcealed intent to destroy an entire portion of the country's population—an intent that was almost completely actualized.

Rwanda is located in East Africa and covers an area of approximately 25,000 square kilometres. It borders on Uganda, the Democratic Republic of Congo, Tanzania, and Rwanda's twin, the country of Burundi, with its strikingly similar traits and problems. A mountainous country with no maritime outlet, Rwanda is located almost 2,000 kilometres from the ports of Mombasa (Kenya) and Dar es

---

[1] According to the UN Genocide Convention genocidal acts are acts committed with the intent of destroying, in whole or in part, national, ethnical, racial or religious groups. War crimes are crimes committed against the international law of war, e.g. killing prisoners of war or enemy soldiers wounded in combat (or refusal to give medical treatment to enemy soldiers). Crimes against humanity are acts committed in times of war or peace, such as mass killings of civilians, large-scale crimes of rape, slavery, etc.

Salaam (Tanzania). It is one of the poorest countries in the world, with virtually no minerals; most of its population (95%) lives in villages and small towns and makes a livelihood from agriculture. Primary crops for self-consumption include bananas and sweet potatoes, and the primary crops for export are coffee and tea. In 1994, the population of Rwanda stood at 7.2 million, and the country's population density was amongst the highest in Africa. Rwanda is not only the least urbanized country in Africa but also the country with the slowest rate of urbanization on the continent (between 1954 and 1994, the country's urban population increased from 1% to 5%). The per capita GNP of this very poor country is one of the lowest in the

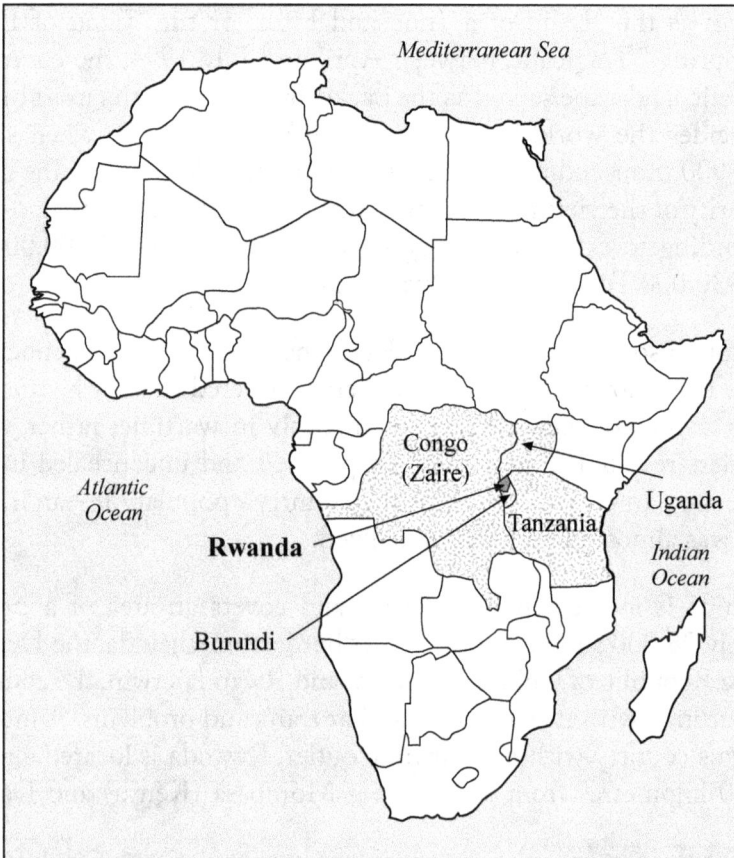

Map 1: Location of Rwanda in Africa

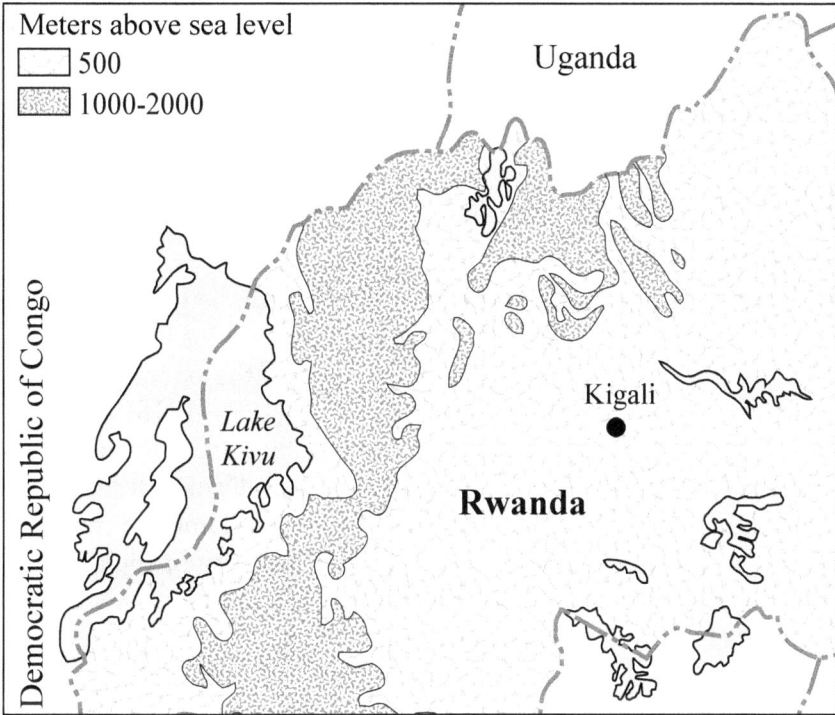

Map 2: Topography of Rwanda

world, and the average life expectancy is less than fifty years. Nonetheless, in comparison to other African countries, the Rwandan population in 1994 was relatively educated, with a 50% literacy rate (64% among men and 37% among women). Certain aspects of its infrastructure, such as electricity and roads, are also relatively efficient compared to other African countries.

In 1994, Rwanda's population consisted of three ethnic groups: Hutu (85%), Tutsi (14%), and Twa (1%). Although the Hutu and Tutsi are to some extent physiognomically different, culturally and linguistically they have always regarded themselves as members of the same group. They both refer to themselves as Banyarwanda and speak Kinyarwanda, one of the Bantu languages, which are widely spoken throughout eastern and central Africa.[2] As a result of Bel-

---

2 In Bantu languages, the prefix *"ki"* means "language" and the prefix *"ba"* or *"wa"* means many. Based on this etymology, the word Banyarwanda refers to the people of Rwanda, while Kinyarwanda refers to the language of the people of Rwanda.

gium's extended rule in Rwanda (1916–1962), French also became the official language of the country, serving as the language of government and of high-school and university education. Still, Kinyarwanda remains the most widely spoken language.

For centuries, most (but not all) of the inhabitants of Rwanda shared a country and, as subjects of one kingdom and one king, a common history.[3] Nor are Hutu and Tutsi separated by any major religious differences. In both groups the majority is Catholic (approximately 65%), and the minority is Protestant (20%) or Muslim (10%). As a result of intense missionary activity, most of the population converted to Christianity under both German (1898–1916) and Belgian (1916–1962) rule. Previously, the inhabitants of Rwanda had practiced traditional African religions. Hutu and Tutsi attended the same churches and schools. They lived in similar homes, in the same neighbourhoods and villages, and the vast majority of their people was extremely poor (although Tutsi typically accounted for a higher percentage of the socioeconomic upper class).

Nevertheless, despite the common traits they share, the two populations actually constitute two distinct ethnic groups with unique perceptions of their separate origins, and a strong sense of differentiation that encouraged the establishment of separate communal identities. (The scholarly literature tends to regard ethnicity as not necessarily rooted in "objective" facts, but rather in assessments that are "subjective" by nature, and based on feelings of solidarity, self-identity, and common interests).

Members of the third group, the Twa, which is significantly smaller than the other two, are physically distinct from the Tutsi and the Hutu. They also speak their own unique dialect of Kinyarwanda and practice either traditional religion or Christianity. All Twa were originally hunters and gatherers, but later on became labourers and servants of the Hutu and Tutsi. During the months of the 1994 genocide, Twa numbered amongst both the perpetrators and the victims.

---

[3]   For a detailed chronological table of events in Rwandan history between the sixteenth and the early twenty-first century, see Appendix 1.

Ethnic groups typically have common traits that may be objective (e.g. physical features, language, religion, and history) or subjective (e.g. consciousness, solidarity, and emotions) in nature. When ethnic groups strive to become institutionalized politically through statehood or autonomy, they become "ethnonations." In your view, are the Hutu, the Tutsi, and the Twa ethnic groups? Or, might they better be classified as ethno-nations? Compare these groups with Jews in Israel, Palestinians in the West Bank and the Gaza Strip, African Americans in the United States, and Scots in Great Britain.

PRECOLONIAL RWANDA

To be a Tutsi was thus to be in power, near power, or simply to be identified with power—just as to be a Hutu was more and more to be a subject.

(Mamdani 2001, 75)

The precolonial Kingdom of Rwanda was established in the sixteenth century through the interaction of three groups: the Hutu, the Tutsi, and the Twa (Newbury 1988, 95). According to most scholars, Hutu and Tutsi have maintained a distinct identity for many centuries. They insisted that the Europeans who reached Rwanda in the late nineteenth century found a society that already incorporated this "tribal" division.[4] Nevertheless, the members of the two groups shared a common culture and language, regarding themselves as Banyarwanda and as subjects of one large, shared kingdom. They even served in the same army, and lived in shared residential areas (Prunier 1995; Clapham 1998; Newbury 1998; Uvin 1997; Lemarchand 1996; Mamdani 2001). What many scholars noted, however, was the physical difference between the Hutu, who resemble the Bantu population of Uganda and Tanzania, and the taller,

---

[4]   In colonial terminology, African ethnic groups (e.g. Ibo, Yoruba, Bakongo, Kikuyu, Hutu, or Tutsi) were regarded as "tribes." Similar European groups (e.g. Basques, Scots, Croats, or Slovaks) were called ethnic groups, nationalities, or nations. The distinction can be traced back to European colonial racism.

slimmer, slightly lighter-skinned Tutsi, who resemble the Hamit-ic-Cushitic population of the Horn of Africa. Some also remarked on the cultural differences between the two groups. For example, John Fage, a well-known historian of Africa, found the Tutsi's unique burial customs to differ from those of the Hutu, and to bear greater similarity to those practiced by the Sidama of Ethiopia (Fage 1978). The Tutsi, who constituted the ruling class in the precolonial kingdoms of Rwanda and Burundi, were similar in physical appearance, culture, and historical consciousness to the ruling classes in the kingdoms of Buganda, Bunyoro, and Ankole in Uganda.

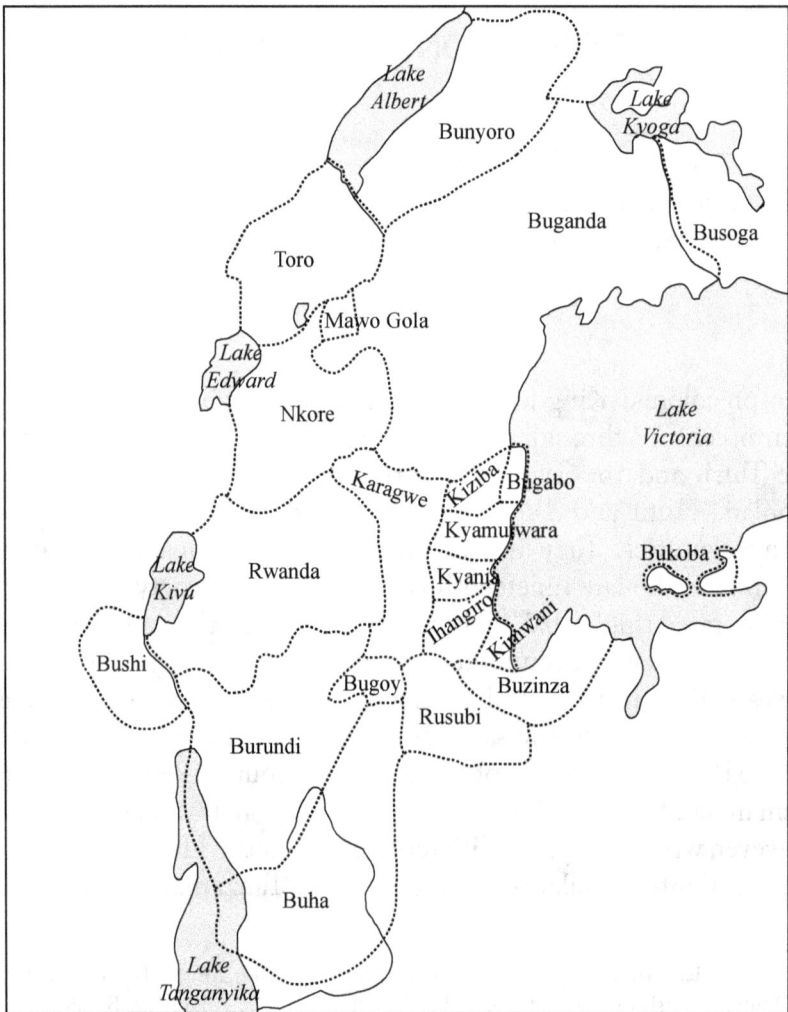

Map 3: The historical kingdoms (1800): Rwanda and its neighbours

In the absence of written histories, the origins of the Hutu, the Tutsi, and the Twa are shrouded in mystery. It can be assumed (although it is not at all certain) that by the time the Tutsi, who according to the Hamitic theory originated from the Horn of Africa, reached the area in the fourteenth or fifteenth century, the Hutu had already migrated there earlier (from the Congo), as had the Twa, apparently the oldest people in the area. As is sometimes the case in Africa, the common language spoken by all three groups may have its roots in the acceptance of the dominant language of the local population by conquerors who were relatively few in number.

In contrast to this, other scholars, such as Alain Destexhe, Catharine Newbury, and Alison Des Forges, maintain that the distinction between Tutsi and Hutu during the precolonial period was not ethnic but rather one of class—the contrast between an elite of ruling cattle herders and the masses they controlled. According to proponents of this school of thought, the class differences only came to be associated with ethnic identity during the colonial period. In other words, the Germans and the Belgians "invented" the respective ethnic identities of the Tutsi and the Hutu. These scholars also hold that the Tutsi did not originally come from the Horn of Africa, as their ethnic origin is identical to that of the Hutu. Instead, they explain the undeniable physical distinctions between the two groups as the product of class-based endogamy (i.e. marriage within a specific group) among the elite and among the masses. Historian Walter Rodney proposes a different explanation for the physical differences between the two groups: the significant nutritional differences between the rich diet enjoyed by the aristocracy and the much poorer diet of the farmers. The confusion in the debate on the ethnic identity of the Hutu and Tutsi is clearly reflected in the following observation of Mahmood Mamdani:

> I was nonplussed to be told over and over again by leading people in the RPF: "We speak the same language, have the same culture, and live on the same hills; we are the same people." But in casual conversation and out in the street, some of the same individuals would readily identify Muhutu and Mututsi. Sometimes by physical appearance. (Pottier 2002, 122)

In any event, the less than convincing explanations offered by this school of thought leave us with the impression that their primary motivation is to prove that colonialism is to blame for all of Rwanda's problems. Although we can assume that the Hutu and Tutsi identities have undergone changes over the years, evidence clearly indicates that there is little truth in the manipulative thesis that colonialism "invented" these two distinctive identities. However, even if we accept the premise that ethnic differentiation did not precede the colonial period, there is no doubt that, throughout the twentieth century, the Hutu and Tutsi had distinct ethnic identities in terms of ethnic consciousness and sentiment, solidarity, and perceptions of "us" and "them."

Interethnic problems notwithstanding, precolonial Rwanda had one major unifying factor: the king (*mwami*). The population believed the king to be a messiah, a savior of the people—of divine origins, infallible and not to be challenged. As far as we know, the king enjoyed the support of all three groups. He ruled his subjects with an iron fist and instituted a tradition of blind obedience, a factor that proved to be extremely important in the unfolding of the 1994 genocide.

Anthropologist Jean-Jacques Maquet characterized the traditional system of rule in Rwanda as follows:

> The role of the ruler was a mixture of protection and paternalistic profit [...] The subject was expected to fit within this form of leadership. He was supposed to adopt a dependent attitude. Inferiority is the relative situation of a person who has to submit to another in a defined field. But dependence is inferiority extended to all spheres of life. *When a ruler gives an order he must be obeyed, not because his order falls into the sphere over which he has authority, but simply because he is the ruler.* (Prunier 1995, 57)

Under the king's ruling, the upper echelon consisted of three different types of chiefs: chiefs of men (*mutwale wa ingabo*), chiefs of the landholdings (*mutwale wa buttaka*), and chiefs of the pastures (*mutwale wa igikingi*). The chiefs, who were mostly Tutsi, ruled the people, the land, and the cattle. This discriminatory rule clearly reflected the hierarchical relationship between Tutsi and Hutu. For example, when a Tutsi killed a Hutu, the king would order the death of one member of the murderer's family. However, when a Hutu killed a Tutsi, the king would order the death of two members of the murderer's family. The same principle applied in property-related crimes: a Tutsi who stole cattle from a Hutu was exempt from paying punitive damages unless the Hutu had a Tutsi patron. In contrast, when a Hutu stole cattle from a Tutsi, it was considered a serious crime.

The cattle herders, all of whom were Tutsi, were the ruling class of the kingdom. The peasants, who were primarily Hutu, belonged to

Illustration 1: Rwandan king Charles Mutara Rudahigwa (ruled 1931–1959)

the lower class. Hutu were prohibited from owning cattle, which in Rwanda was a customary symbol of health, power, and good ancestry. They were forced to fulfill the needs of their Tutsi masters and to provide them with agricultural produce. In return, they received protection. At times, unequal contractual agreements emerged between Tutsi patrons and Hutu subordinates. Such contracts, or *ubuhake*, were sealed by the actual transfer of land and cattle to the Hutu farmer, although officially they remained the property of the Tutsi patron. The right to own cattle and land was hereditary, and always remained with the Tutsi. It was only through this arrangement that Hutu were able to acquire grazing land. According to this system, a Hutu who acquired both his livelihood and the protection of the Tutsi lord became the lord's client (*mugaragu*) and was compelled to work in his fields, provide him with agricultural produce, carry out repairs in his house, and give him

Illustration 2: Tutsi lord and his servant

some of his daughters as concubines. In fact, he was obliged to do whatever the lord commanded (this arrangement remained in place during the colonial period as well). In traditional Rwanda, the Hutu were also engaged in forced labour, while Tutsi—not only members of the oligarchy, but also the poor—were exempt.

Tutsi dominance was institutionalized despite the class-based distinctions found within each group (Figure 1). Although clans consisted of a mixture of Tutsi, Hutu, and Twa, they were based on a clear internal class hierarchy largely consistent with the ethnic divisions (Figure 2). The traditional army was also hierarchically structured: the Tutsi were the warriors and the only recipients of combat training, whereas the Hutu and the Twa served in supporting roles, such as carriers.

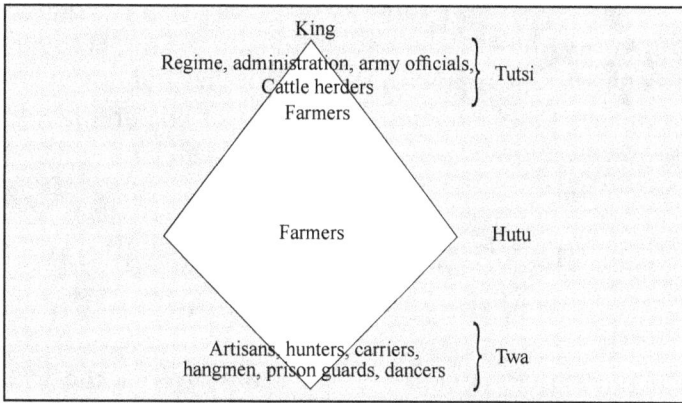

Figure 1: Class structure in traditional Rwanda (Mamdani 2001, 74)

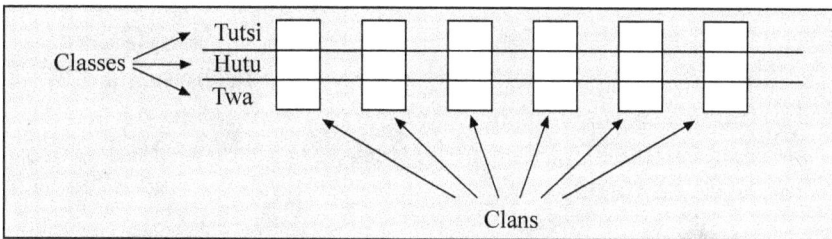

Figure 2: Class hierarchy in traditional Rwanda

There is no consensus among scholars regarding the causes of the bloody conflict between the Hutu and the Tutsi, which reached its height in 1994, when 800,000 of the 930,000 Tutsi living in Rwanda were slaughtered. As we have seen, scholars are also divided on the historical roots of the conflict and the origin of the distinct identities of the Hutu and the Tutsi. Thus, the struggle between the two ethnic groups has spurred a "conflict about the character of the conflict" (Lemarchand 1996, 17).

Whatever the origins of the Hutu and the Tutsi, relations between them were already problematic in the precolonial period. On this basis, we can conclude that tensions were not simply the product of colonialism, as argued by Lemarchand and others (1995, 8–11). It is most likely that the idea of Tutsi dominance, based on divine favor, had been widespread many years before the onset of colonial rule, a conclusion strongly supported by the myth surrounding the establishment of the kingdom. Therefore, when the ethnographers and missionaries first arrived in the region, they did not "invent" the negative images that Tutsi and Hutu held of one another. In their accounts, however, the Europeans may very well have inflated them (Uvin 1996, 6–7).

The Myth of the Establishment of the Earthly Kingdom

> The supreme deity Imana created Kazikamuntu, the forefather of all humans, among whose sons were Gatwa, Gahutu, and Gatutsi, the founding fathers of the Twa, the Hutu, and the Tutsi, respectively. After the first son, Gatwa, killed one of his brothers, he was cursed by his father and fated to be inferior to Gahutu and Gatutsi. When the second son, Gahutu, did not complete some of the tasks he had been assigned by his father, he was punished and became inferior to the third brother, Gatutsi. In this way, Gatutsi was chosen as the first of the three brothers.

The orally transmitted intergenerational historical legacies studied by Belgian anthropologist and historian Jan Vansina indicate that in the precolonial period Hutu and Tutsi were not in a state of ongoing warfare, and certainly did not engage in rioting, massacres, and genocidal acts like those that took place from the 1960s onward (Lemarchand 1996, 11). There is thus no justification for speaking of the "eruption" of "ancient tribal hatred" in Rwanda and Burundi in the 1990s. Such claims result from reading history backward, based on events that took place in the second half of the twentieth century. In fact, in the seventeenth, eighteenth, and nineteenth centuries, internal wars among the various Tutsi dynasties and acts of violence among the mixed clans were much more prevalent than wars between the Hutu and the Tutsi (Newbury 1988).

TRADITIONAL RWANDA AND COLONIAL RWANDA

The territories of the traditional Kingdom of Rwanda and the colonial territory of Rwanda (1898–1962), which in 1962 emerged as the independent state of Rwanda, did not completely overlap. Still, the bulk of the territory controlled by colonial Rwanda during the era of German occupation (1898–1916) had previously been ruled by the traditional Rwandan kingdom of Kigeri IV Rwabugiri (ruled 1860–1895). The few areas in which there was no territorial overlap were in northwestern Rwanda (as per its colonial borders), in which three relatively small Hutu kingdoms had been established in the eighteenth century. These areas were fully annexed to the traditional Rwandan kingdom only in the colonial period: the Kingdom of Kibari in 1918, the Kingdom of Bushiru in 1920, and the Kingdom of Bukonya in 1931 (Prunier 1995, 7). In contrast to the traditional kingdom, the rulers of these smaller kingdoms were Hutu, and the few Tutsi who lived within their borders enjoyed no political power whatsoever.

The significant differences between the northwestern region and the other parts of Rwanda will be discussed further on, as we recount the events leading up to the genocide of 1994. Here, we will only note that Juvénal Habyarimana, the president of Rwanda between 1973 and 1994, and his close associates regarded themselves as the progeny of the princes of the northern Kingdom of Bushiru, and were known by all as "northern Hutu." It is interesting to note that the chief instigators of the 1994 genocide included a prominent

Rwandan intellectual and historian, Professor Ferdinand Nahimana of the National University of Rwanda, who had studied the Hutu kingdoms of the northwest, located in the administrative districts of Ruhengeri and Gisenyi (see map 4).

Map 4: The Ruhengeri and Gisenyi districts in Rwanda

In addition to the traditional kingdom and the areas that were annexed to colonial Rwanda in 1918, concentrations of Banyarwanda (Kinyarwanda-speaking Hutu and Tutsi) also lived in areas of the African Great Lakes Region, which were subsequently incorporated into Uganda and the Belgian Congo (today's Democratic Republic of Congo). Later on, in 1928–1929 and again in 1946, large-scale starvation in Rwanda led to mass emigration of Banyarwanda to the Belgian Congo.

Nevertheless, the territories controlled by colonial and independent Rwanda were, to a large degree, identical to the territories controlled by traditional Rwanda. Rwanda therefore differs markedly from most African countries, which were artificially constructed during the colonial era. From this perspective, Rwanda is nevertheless similar to a small group of African countries, including Burundi, Swaziland, Lesotho, and Ethiopia, which also have roots in historic precolonial kingdoms.

Lake Kivu

Rwanda

Congo (Zaire)

Lake Tanganyika

Burundi

Map 5: Banyarwanda (Kinyarwanda speakers) in the Great Lakes Region

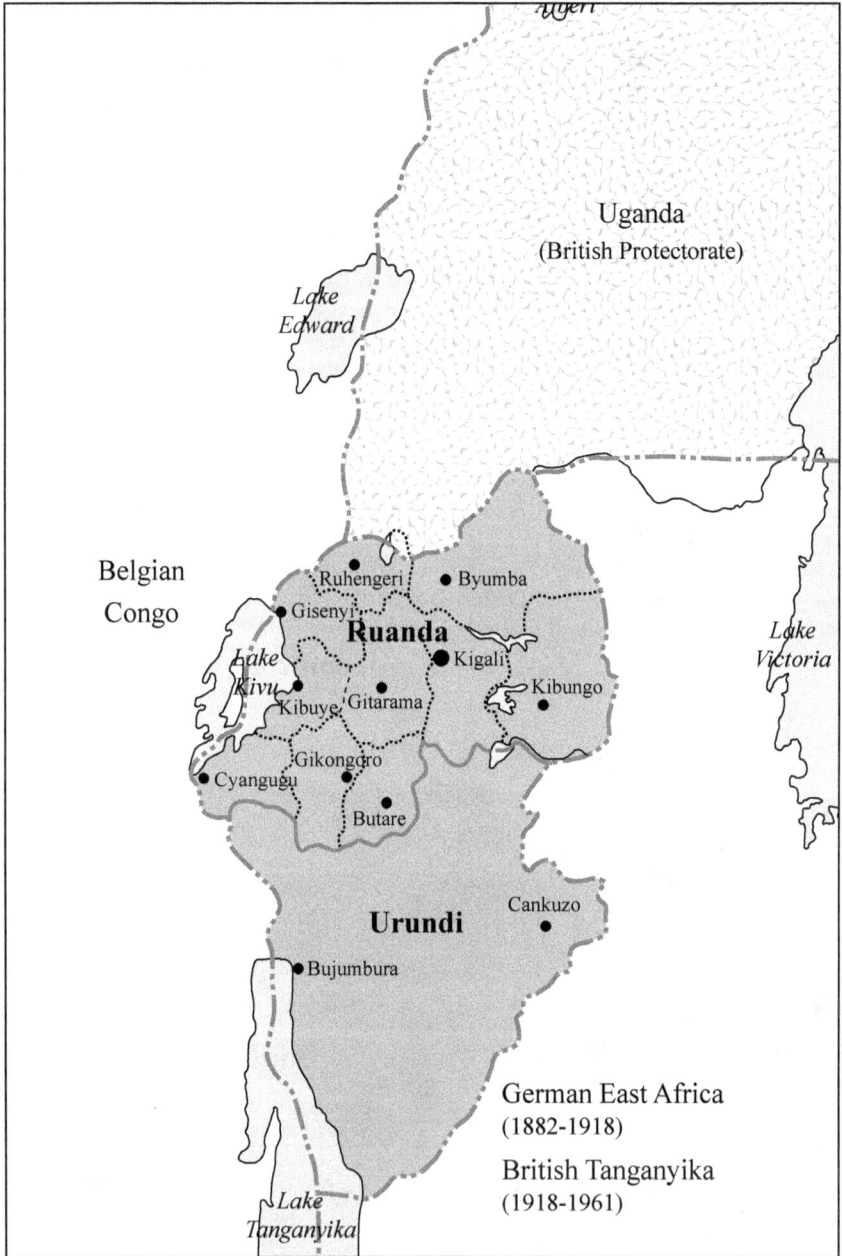

Map 6: The Great Lakes Region after World War I

THE COLONIAL PERIOD (1898-1962)

Rwanda's relatively short colonial history can be divided into two periods: that of German rule (1898–1916) and that of Belgian rule (1916–1962).[5] The Germans considered "Ruanda" (German spelling of Rwanda) along with the Kingdom of Urundi (today Burundi)—together known as Ruanda-Urundi—as part of German East Africa, most of which subsequently became British Tanganyika (and which today constitutes mainland Tanzania). The colonial borders of Ruanda-Urundi were based on the traditional precolonial borders of the two kingdoms. In practice, the traditional kingdoms of Rwanda and Urundi persisted throughout the colonial period. Since the system of government was one of indirect rule,[6] the Germans and the Belgians needed very few governors, officials, clerks, or soldiers to maintain their rule.

In 1914, a total of ninety-six Germans (including all colonial officials, soldiers, missionaries, and merchants) governed German "Ruanda," a territory more than twice the size of Belgium. In certain respects, the traditional Kingdom of Rwanda was strengthened during the colonial period as a result of the conquest and annexation of the northwestern Hutu kingdoms.

The colonial period witnessed the onset of mass conversions to Christianity across Africa. Christian missionaries made church membership a precondition for entry into the colonial elite, or to be more precise, into the second tier of the colonial elite, as the most senior positions were consistently occupied by Europeans. During Belgian rule, Catholicism became something of an official religion in Rwanda. Western education was under the complete control of

---

[5] Although officially the Allies controlled Rwanda between 1916 and 1918, Belgium was actually the dominant force in the country during this period. The all-Belgian regime that ruled the country from 1918 onward was institutionalized in 1924 as a mandate of the League of Nations. After World War II, the mandate became a UN trusteeship territory.

[6] Indirect rule: a form of colonial rule by which European powers ruled with the help of local traditional rulers. This system was based on the premise that it was the most efficient and inexpensive form of rule and would result in the least tension with the local population.

Christian missionaries and the only practical avenue of higher education available to Africans at the time was training for the clergy.

Colonialism was marked by regime brutality against the local population. The Germans and Belgians alike employed large-scale forced labour in agriculture (coffee and potato cultivation), in the construction of mountain slope terraces, the paving of roads, and the erection of public buildings. During Belgian rule in general, and in particular throughout the two world wars, men were required to spend more than half their work time in forced labour. Africans who refused to report for work were brutally punished, and as a result hundreds of thousands fled to the neighbouring British-controlled territories of Uganda and Tanganyika. Such forced-labour projects can be understood as a joint venture of the colonial rulers and the local chiefs, since they provided both with power and material benefits. Because the chiefs and their assistants were Tutsi who exercised control over the Hutu forced labourers with whiplashes, intense animosity between the two groups escalated during this period.

To understand the impact of colonialism on Hutu-Tutsi relations, we must first understand the manner in which the colonial rulers viewed the local population. The following excerpts from representatives of the colonial government are reflective of this perspective. One Belgian clergyman described the Tutsi as follows:

> We can see Caucasian skulls and beautiful Greek profiles side by side with Semitic and even Jewish features, elegant golden-red beauties in the heart of Ruanda and Urundi. (Prunier 1995, 7)

Another clergyman wrote:

> The Bahima [a Tutsi clan] differ absolutely by the beauty of their features and their light color from the Bantu agriculturalists of an inferior type. Tall and well proportioned, they have long thin noses, a wide brow and fine lips. They say they came from the North. Their intelligent and delicate appearance, their love of money, their capacity to adapt to any situation seem to indicate a Semitic origin. (Prunier 1995, 7–8)

In 1927, the Belgian governor of Rwanda addressed the different leadership capacities of the members of the two groups, and concluded decisively:

The Batutsi were meant to reign. Their fine presence is in itself enough to give them great prestige vis-à-vis the inferior races which surround them [...] It is not surprising that those good Bahutu, less intelligent, more simple, more spontaneous, more trusting, have let themselves be enslaved without ever daring to revolt. (Prunier 1995, 7–8)

RACE THEORY
DURING THE COLONIAL PERIOD

Even before the institutionalization of German rule in Rwanda, European explorers who reached the area in the late nineteenth century had developed theories of Tutsi superiority and Hutu inferiority, which were consistent with the Western spirit of the time. The nineteenth and twentieth centuries were eras of race theories that were widespread in Germany, Britain, the United States, France, and Belgium. Without awareness of the race theory that was prevalent in Rwanda at the time, it is impossible to understand the events of 1994.

Joseph Arthur Comte de Gobineau's *Essai sur l'inégalité des races humaines* (*An Essay on the Inequality of the Human Races*) was extremely influential at the time.[7] In 1863, a similar position was adopted by the explorer of the Nile, John Hanning Speke, in his *Theory of Conquest of Inferior by Superior Races*. According to Speke, the ruling groups in the kingdoms of the Great Lakes Region (including Rwanda and Burundi) belonged to a "superior civilization," with roots in the partly Christian and partly Muslim Galla people of Ethiopia (the largest ethnic group in Ethiopia, accounting for approximately 40% of the population, now known as Oromo).[8]

---

[7] Joseph Arthur Comte de Gobineau (1816–1882) was a French thinker who played a major role in developing modern race theory. In his book, *An Essay on the Inequality of the Human Races* (1853–1855), he classified humanity into inferior and superior races. The inferior races included the yellow race, which he described as "materialist" and "uncreative," and the black race, which he described as "unintelligent" and "crude." In his view, the degeneration of the "mixed" Jewish race was the result of its mixing with "black elements." In France, de Gobineau identified a link between the French upper class and its "German-Frankish racial quality."

[8] Speke is thought to have discovered the source of the Nile River in Lake Victoria after undertaking a journey from East Africa to the lake, along the Nile River to Gondo Koro, and from there to Cairo.

Similar theories were developed by other scholars and explorers, such as Sir Samuel Baker, Gaetano Casati, Sir Harry Johnston, Father Léon Classe, and Father François Ménard. Among other things, they posited that the Tutsi were the progeny of Shem or Ham, and that they hailed from Ethiopia or ancient Egypt, Asia Minor, the Caucuses, India, or Tibet. According to these writers, the Tutsi are pictured as "coloured whites," as "Europeans under a black skin," as members of a "superior race," similar in appearance to the ancient Romans.

Each of these authors applied the full gamut of racist European stereotypes to the Hutu, not to mention the Twa. Like all Africans, they were perceived as passive, lazy, ugly, and primitive. The Tutsi, in contrast, were portrayed as handsome, proud, hard working, loyal, intelligent, and politically adept, and therefore as not African in character. In this way, the descriptions offered by the European explorers and researchers of the nineteenth century were consistent with European race theory, which regarded Africans as an inferior race of the lowest order (Clapham 1998; Hintjens 1999).

During German and Belgian colonial rule, race theory continued to develop and gain influence. The influence of the racial approach was reflected in everyday accounts written by colonial government officials, as in the following excerpts, taken from Belgian colonial reports from 1925:

Description of the Twa
Member of a worn out and quickly disappearing race [...] the Mutwa present a number of well-defined somatic characteristics: he is small, chunky, muscular, and very hairy; particularly on the chest. With a monkey-like flat face and a huge nose, he is quite similar to the apes whom he chases in the forest.

Description of the Hutu
The Bahutu display very typical Bantu features [...] They are generally short and thick-set with a big head, a jovial expression, a wide nose, and enormous lips. They are extroverts who like to laugh and lead a simple life.

Description of the Tutsi
The Mututsi of good race has nothing of the negro, apart from his colour. He is usually very tall, 1.80 m. at least, often 1.90 m. or more. He is very thin, a characteristic which tends to be even more noticeable as he gets older. His features are very fine: a high brow, thin nose and fine lips

framing beautiful shining teeth. Batutsi women are usually lighter-skinned than their husbands, very slender and pretty in their youth, although they tend to thicken with age. Gifted with a vivacious intelligence, the Tutsi displays a refinement of feelings which is rare among primitive people. He is a natural-born leader, capable of extreme self-control and of calculated goodwill. (Prunier 1995, 6)

As noted, the racial theories that evolved in Europe during the nineteenth century and gained control over twentieth-century colonial thought were clearly reflected in colonial policies applied in Rwanda: the point of departure of the Germans and the Belgians who gained control of the country was that its population could and should be understood as a pyramid of different races (see Figure 3).

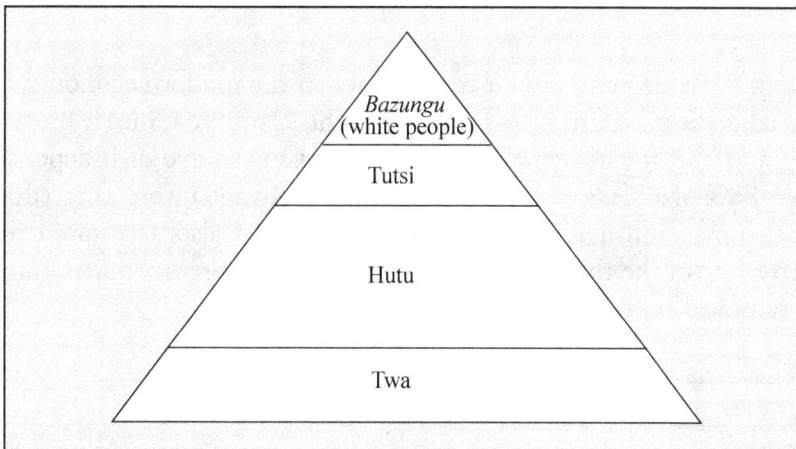

Figure 3: The breakdown of races in colonial Rwanda

In accordance with this approach, almost all the chiefs recognized by the colonial authorities were Tutsi. In 1938, the Belgian bishop Monseigneur Léon Classe made a compelling case for this policy:

The greatest mistake this government could make would be to suppress the Mututsi caste. Such a revolution would lead the country directly to anarchy and to hateful anti-European communism [...] We will have no better, more active and more intelligent chiefs than the Batutsi. They are the ones best suited to understand progress and the ones the population likes best. *The government must work mainly with them.* (Prunier 1995, 6)

In 1929, the Belgians decided to combine the roles of the different types of chiefs, who according to the traditional power structure
outlined above controlled the people, the land, and the cattle. This
resulted in the dismissal of most of the Hutu chiefs. Table 1 shows
the numerical division of chiefs between Tutsi and Hutu at the end
of the colonial period.

Chiefs	Tutsi	Hutu
Chiefs (chefs de chefferies)	43	2
Subchiefs (sous-chefs)	549	10

Table 1: Hutu and Tutsi chiefs, 1959 (Prunier 1995, 27)

Many Tutsi also enjoyed clear privileges in the modern economy, in
the education system (see Table 2), in the Catholic Church hierarchy, and the government administration. On the eve of independence, 88% of all African colonial officials in Rwanda were Tutsi (due,
among other things, to their education). Tutsi also accounted for
thirty-one of the thirty-three members of the Supreme State Council (Conseil supérieur du pays).

Year	Group	
	Tutsi	Hutu
1932	45	9
1945	46	3
1954	63	19 (16 of whom were from Burundi)
1959	279	143

Table 2: Hutu and Tutsi students at Astrida College (Prunier 1995, 33)

Northwestern Rwanda, which had never been part of the traditional kingdom, was ruled by a brutally repressive Belgian-Tutsi regime. In this region, Hutu chiefs were ousted, and were replaced by Tutsi governors, the land holdings of privileged Hutu dynasties were expropriated and transferred to the kingdom, and the Hutu were subjected to forced labour requirements on a larger scale than in the past. It comes as no surprise, then, that this was one of the many sources of tension during the Hutu Revolution of 1959 (see below) and in the days of the "final solution" in 1994.

In 1933, the Belgians began the practice of recording ethnic identity (ubwoko) on identity cards, an additional measure that ultimately (although clearly inadvertently) played a lethal role in shaping the events of 1994. The authorities regarded as Tutsi all individuals who possessed at least ten cows, who had been registered as Tutsi by the church, or were Tutsi in appearance. The rest of the population was registered as either Hutu or Twa, in accordance with their occupation and appearance (Mamdani 2001, 99). According to this administrative process, the population of Rwanda in 1933 was 84% Hutu, 15% Tutsi, and 1% Twa. This formal process reflected the relationship between class and ethnicity, even though it was allegedly based on class distinctions only (since it was based on people's occupations, with cattle herders having higher status than farmers, and on the number of head of cattle owned). The addition of ethnicity to Rwandan identity cards reinforced ethnic categorizations, for, despite typical distinctions, a significant number of Tutsi and Hutu were physically quite indistinguishable from one another. In such cases, ethnic identity was based on official registration.

It should be noted that a degree of class mobility did exist in traditional Rwanda, when individual Hutu could acquire Tutsi status (if they accumulated sufficient power and wealth), and individual Tutsi could be brought down to the status of Hutu (if they lost their cattle, became farmers, or married Hutu women, for instance). The ethnic registration of 1933 put an end to this social mobility (Mamdani 2001, 101).

The same process also halted the growth of a mixed population known as "Hutsis," which until then had grown steadily. Children were now registered in accordance with the recorded ethnic identity of their fathers, even if their mothers belonged to a different ethnic group. As a result, decades later, during the 1994 genocide, people with Tutsi fathers and Hutu mothers were slaughtered, while people with Hutu fathers and Tutsi mothers at times managed to survive.

During the colonial period, Hutu-Tutsi relations also deteriorated as a result of the widespread absorption by both groups of colonial race theories regarding the superiority of the Tutsi and the inferiority of the Hutu. Many Tutsi—including the poor majority known as "small Tutsi" (les petits tutsis)—believed that they were the offspring of Ham and, as a result of this lineage, regarded themselves as superior to the Hutu. For their part, the Hutu regarded the Tutsi as foreign invaders, "Ethiopians," who were imposing oppressive and exploitative rule on them.

Naturally, the hatred of Tutsi "feudalism" and "colonialism" that emerged among the Hutu reinforced their own ethnic identity. As in many other well-known cases, once the colonial narrative enters the history books, it assumes the status of objective fact.

Consider the differences and similarities between traditional Rwanda and colonial Rwanda. Focus primarily on regime structure, prevailing ideology, social policies, and the status of Hutu and Tutsi.

THE HUTU REVOLUTION (1959-1962)

The winds of change that began to blow across Africa in the 1950s had far-reaching impact on the Hutu and Tutsi elite. In 1957, nine prominent Hutu intellectuals published the Bahutu Manifesto (Le manifeste des Bahutu), which contained a call to break the political, economic, and social monopoly of the Tutsi.

The Hutu intellectuals demanded "democratic majority rule," removal of the "racist-colonialist Tutsi system," and the return of Tutsi "colonizers" to Ethiopia. One Hutu leader even called for the removal of the symbol of the sacred royal drums, the kalinga, which were decorated with the desiccated testicles of Hutu princes who had been defeated in past wars.

The king's court rejected the Hutu demands out of hand. According to the royalists, the legitimacy of the Tutsi monarchy stemmed from their military victory and the establishment of the kingdom itself. Instead, they demanded "immediate independence" from the Belgians in order to prevent completion of the democratization process, which threatened to transfer rule to the Hutu majority prior to the achievement of full independence.

Ironically, the Tutsi oligarchy received the backing of the United Nations, the Communist bloc, and the Third World.[9] At the same time, the radical revolutionary demands of the Hutu were not supported by "progressive circles" because they did not include a call for "immediate independence." (It is interesting to note that something similar took place in Zanzibar at the time, when the Arab aristocracy demanding immediate independence was backed by Gamal Abdul Nasser of Egypt,[10] and Kwame Nkrumah of Ghana,[11] while the African majority, which sought a power reversal prior to independence, received the support of neither East nor West.)

How do the concepts of democratization, decolonization, and revolution apply to the case of Rwanda?

---

[9]   The term oligarchy is derived from the Greek word for "rule of the few." Aristotle used the term to mean "rule of the few in their own interests." Today, the term is typically used to refer to a ruling elite made up of large estates holders, leading capitalists, nouveaux riches, or military commanders who use the ruling regime as a mechanism to enrich themselves.

[10]   Gamal Abdul Nasser (1918–1970) was president of Egypt between 1956 and 1970 and widely supported throughout the Arab world. His image as a bulwark against colonialism inspired the masses within and outside Egypt, as did his call for Arab unity under his leadership. He announced his resignation after Egypt's military defeat in the Arab-Israeli war of 1967, but Egyptian public opinion stopped him from leaving office until his death in September 1970.

[11]   Kwame Nkrumah (1909–1972) was the president of Ghana between 1957 and 1966. In 1947, he founded the anticolonialist Convention People's Party (CPP). After his party's victory in the elections of 1951, he was appointed prime minister and led the colony to independence in 1957, making it the first colony in Africa to achieve this status. Nkrumah's regime degenerated into a single-party dictatorship and he was ousted from power by a military coup in 1966. He died six years later while in exile in Guinea.

The 1950s also witnessed the formation of distinct Hutu and Tutsi political parties that, from their inception, were based squarely on ethnic identity. In 1957, southern Hutu established the Association for the Social Advancement of the Masses (*Association pour la promotion sociale des masses*) or APROSOMA,[12] a relatively moderate Hutu party under the leadership of businessman Joseph Gitera. During the same period, ethnic Hutu from northwest and central Rwanda (the districts of Gitarama and Ruhengeri) established the Hutu Social Movement (*Mouvement social Muhutu*) or the MSM, which in 1959 became the Democratic Republican Movement, the Party for the Emancipation of the Hutu (*Mouvement démocratique républicain—parti du mouvement de l'émancipation Hutu*), or MDR-Parmehutu.

In the Tutsi camp, 1959 marked the establishment of the Rwandan National Union (Union nationale rwandaise), or the UNAR, a monarchist anti-Belgian party calling for immediate decolonization. In response, the Belgians encouraged the establishment of the Democratic Assembly of Rwanda (Rassemblement démocratique rwandais), or RADER, an ethnic Tutsi party with moderate positions toward both the Belgians and the Hutu.

Between 1959 and 1962, Rwanda underwent a full-scale revolution: the Hutu removed the Tutsi from power, the traditional monarchy was dissolved, and the country achieved independence from the Belgians. The revolution went by many names: *muyaga*, Kinyarwandan for a "strong and erratic wind"; the "Hutu Revolution"; the "social revolution"; the "democratic revolution" (as it was called by the Hutu); and the "slaughter and the riots" (as called by the Tutsi).

---

[12]   Like the names of all political parties in Rwanda, the party's name is French. Under Belgian rule, this was the language of the governing regime, the administration, the education system, and the intelligentsia.

Position	Hutu	Tutsi
Moderate	APROSOMA	RADER
Extremist	MDR-Parmehutu	UNAR

Table 3: Political parties in Rwanda (1960)

Consider other historical events that have been classified in different, and in some cases contradictory, terms by the groups and individuals involved.

Despite the independent organization, heightened political awareness, and formation of political parties among the Hutu of Rwanda, it was a change in Belgian policy that finally made the 1959 Hutu Revolution possible. In the 1950s, the Belgians began to withdraw their support for the Tutsi, based on their decision to abandon the feudal-aristocratic Tutsi minority and join the Hutu "democratic majority." This policy change was consistent with the democratic atmosphere that prevailed in Europe in the 1950s, as well as the Belgians' anger at having been "betrayed" by the Tutsi, who now demanded "immediate independence" in order to forestall a preindependence democratic transformation.

An interesting explanation for this change in Belgian policy is related to the history and politics of Belgium itself. Whereas most past colonial officials had been French-speaking Belgian Walloons, things began to change in the 1950s, when an increasing number of Dutch-speaking Flemish arrived in Rwanda. The Flemish regarded the Walloons (and upper-class Flemish who had undergone French cultural assimilation) as a condescending elite and viewed the Tutsi in Rwanda in a similar light. In this context, they were naturally inclined to support the "people," namely the Hutu.

A similar transformation took place within the Catholic Church in Rwanda. Whereas in the 1930s, most priests and conservative missionaries were from the upper class, in the 1950s they were from the lower-middle class and the working class, and were even referred to as le petit clergé (minor clergy). For this reason, the clergy had a natural class-based inclination to support the Hutu masses. In addition, as a result of the Africanization of the clergy, Hutu began pressuring the church to change its policy, resulting in the appointment of a growing number of Hutu priests.

Another important reason for the policy change of the Catholic Church was the work of the Protestant churches among the Hutu population. Hutu tended to associate the Catholic Church with the Tutsi regime and were aware of the dominance of the Tutsi clergy. They therefore tended to join other churches, such as the Baptist and Anglican Churches. In an effort to contend with this dynamic and to forestall a mass movement of Hutu to the Protestant churches, the Catholic Church began to support the Hutu and to appoint an increasing number of Hutu clergymen.

Summarize the reasons for the policy reversal of the Belgian regime and the Catholic Church.

Like many other revolutions throughout history, the revolution that began on November 1, 1959 commenced with an event of seemingly marginal importance. On that day, a group of ruffians from the UNAR attacked a Hutu chief who was active in Parmehutu. In response, Parmehutu members began attacking Tutsi throughout Rwanda, looting and burning their homes. In a large part of northwestern Rwanda, the result was expulsion of the ethnic Tutsi and the effective loss of power of the royal regime in the area. In the course of riots that continued until 1961, 20,000 Tutsi were killed, and some 120,000 fled for their lives to Uganda, Tanganyika, Congo, and Burundi.

As the violent Hutu rebellion against the Tutsi regime was underway, the Belgian government, now a staunch and open supporter of the Hutu, organized a political, so-called democratic and legal, reversal of power: in 1961, the Belgians dismissed all Tutsi chiefs and replaced them with Hutu, who immediately began to persecute the Tutsi and encourage mass violence against them.

A similar power reversal took place on the level of local government.

In the first elections organized by the Belgian government in June 1960, the Hutu gained control of most positions (see Table 4 for detailed election results).

Of the 229 commune heads (in Flemish, *burgemeesters*) elected, 219 were Hutu and 160 were members of Parmehutu. With Belgian encouragement, 3,125 local mayors and council members met in January 1961 to decide on the establishment of the "sovereign and democratic Republic of Rwanda." The Tutsi King Kigeri V was overthrown, and exiled to Uganda.

Party	Group	Position	Number of Representatives
Parmehutu	Hutu	Extremist	2,390 (76.5%)
APROSOMA	Hutu	Moderate	233 (7.4%)
RADER	Tutsi	Moderate	209 (6.7%)
UNAR	Tutsi	Extremist	56 (1.8%)
Independents	Hutu and Tutsi	—	237 (7.6%)

Table 4: Local mayors and Council members, elections of 1960

The parliamentary elections held in June 1961 were an additional step in the revolution, giving Parmehutu 78% and the UNAR 17% of the seats. The election results reflected not only the Hutu's seizure of power, but also the increasing ethnic polarization that now gripped the country, resulting in the disappearance of the moderate parties of APROSOMA and RADER from the parliamentary map. In an effort to underscore the unquestioned legitimacy of the abolition of the monarchy, a referendum was held in September 1961, in which 80% of the voters proved to be in favor of the move.

With Rwandan independence in 1962 and Hutu seizure of power, systematic persecution initiated by the new government took the place of spontaneous attacks against Tutsi. In response to the penetration of Tutsi fighters from Uganda into Rwanda in December 1961, the new Hutu government began referring to the Tutsi as *inyenzi*, or cockroaches. This was a sign of things to come: an estimated 30,000 Tutsi were murdered between 1962 and 1964, and another 200,000 became refugees in neighbouring countries.

Following the events of 1959–1962, including the 1961 elections, Rwanda's Hutu majority came to power for the first time. The new regime put the final touches to the revolution by abolishing the forced labor that until then had been required of the Hutu, and by dispossessing some Tutsi notables of their land in order to redestribute it to Hutu farmers. In practice, the revolution transformed Rwanda into a de facto Hutu state.

Assuming that democratization is linked to free elections, majority rule, the rule of law, equality before the law, and the institution of human and civil rights, can the events that took place in Rwanda between 1959 and 1962 be seen as a transition from authoritarian rule to democracy?

THE FIRST REPUBLIC (1962–1973)

If the Tutsi ever seek to obtain political power again
they will find that the whole Tutsi race will be wiped out.

(Grégoire Kayibanda[13] in Grünfeld and Huijboom 2007, 31)

We are expected to defend ourselves. The only way to go
about [it] is to paralyze the Tutsi. How? They must be
killed.[14]

(Mamdani 2001, 130)

Rwanda gained formal independence on July 1, 1962. Its first president was Grégoire Kayibanda, a Hutu leader (whose wife, incidentally, was a Tutsi). Born to a family of farmers in 1924 and affiliated with the Catholic Church, Kayibanda was a teacher, an editor of the church journal, head of a Catholic commune, and one of the authors

---

[13]   President of Rwanda, 1964.

[14]   Gikongoro Prefect, 1963.

of the Bahutu Manifesto. As the leader of Parmehutu, Kayibanda represented the Hutu of central Rwanda (the Gitarama region), not the more extremist Hutu of the north. The government he established in Rwanda was a de facto Hutu dictatorship.

Kayibanda's rule was no less authoritarian than that of the Tutsi. In fact, despite being referred to as a republic, the new Rwandan regime was actually an autocratic, quasi-monarchist system in democratic-republican guise. All-important positions—government ministers, governors, prefects, commune heads (burgemeesters), and senior officials—were filled by presidential appointment. Strict censorship was enforced on the media by both the state and the church. Because the ruling regime presented itself as puritanical and Christian, draconian punishments were instituted for so-called moral transgressions such as prostitution. In addition, Tutsi political leaders were executed, as were a number of Hutu opposition leaders. The regime prohibited all opposition parties, and relied solely on the support of the sole legal party, the Catholic Church, and on the Belgians, who remained influential even after the Hutu Revolution. Tutsi had no presence in either the army or the police force and were subject to a policy of discrimination in schools, universities, the public administration, and the business world. Ethnic quotas were instituted within the education system and the public administration, and whenever the number of Tutsi exceeded the quota, "corrections" were proposed by "purification committees," serving many Hutu personal interests in filling the positions. Because Tutsi had enjoyed a strong presence in the church education system under colonial rule, "Hutuizing" the education system required government intervention and was achieved through government control of the processes of student enrollment and the hiring of teachers. The government also continued the practice of registering ethnic identity on personal identity cards, thereby preventing members of the Tutsi minority from concealing their identity in order to evade discriminatory policies.

Year	Regime	Tutsi students
1932–1959	Belgium	80–95%
1970	First Republic	40%
1986	Second Republic	14%

Table 5: Proportion of Tutsi students in higher-education institutions

Ideologically, the regime was committed to what it referred to as "true democracy," which in reality meant Hutu rule. It repeatedly asserted that Rwanda belonged to the Hutu and that under the previous Tutsi regime, the country had been under "foreign rule." The government, for its part, incited against the Tutsi and encouraged acts of violence against them, causing hundreds of thousands to flee for their lives.

The two most brutal waves of repression and violence took place in early 1964 (after the Hutu government repulsed the Tutsi who had invaded the country from across the Ugandan border the previous year) and in 1972 (after the mass murder of Hutu by the Tutsi regime in neighbouring Burundi).

Despite the government's discriminatory and repressive anti-Tutsi policies, hundreds of thousands of Tutsi remained in Rwanda, continuing to play a prominent role in commerce, industry, and the free professions. Now, however, they enjoyed no political power, as all Tutsi parties and organizations had been declared illegal.

Although Hutu rule in Rwanda was total, only a small oligarchic echelon benefited from it. The Hutu masses continued to suffer from repression and dire poverty, even after the Hutu Revolution.

Consider the extent to which the events that took place in Rwanda between 1959 and 1962 constituted a revolution. If they can be thought of as a revolution, was it political, social, or ethnic in nature?

On July 5, 1973, Kayibanda's rule came to an end as a result of opposition to his rule within Hutu society. The army, which consisted primarily of northern Hutu who had until then been kept on the margins of the president's regime, staged a military coup. This was the context in which Chief of Staff General Juvénal Habyarimana, who had also served as defence minister under Kayibanda, rose to power.

THE SECOND REPUBLIC (1973-1994)

Beyond its regional dimension (northern Hutu versus southern Hutu), the military coup of 1973 also reflected the adoption of a more hawkish stance toward the Tutsi. We can assume that the radicalization towards the Tutsi resulted from, among others, the massacre of Hutu carried out by Tutsi in 1972 in the neighbouring country of Burundi. In any event, those who carried out the coup regarded the Kayibanda regime as being too "soft" on the Tutsi. It is no coincidence that Habyarimana's associates spoke openly of the 1973 revolution as of a "moral revolution," and not a "social" or "national" revolution, as the 1959 revolution had been dubbed.

What was to be called the "Second Republic," established by General Habyarimana, was the only totalitarian regime of its kind in Africa. It was a single-party regime, controlled by the National Revolutionary Movement for Development (Mouvement révolutionaire pour le développement or MRND), which was established in 1974 and officially declared the only ruling party in 1978. All citizens were forced to become party members, including children and babies. The president of the country was the leader of the party, while government ministers, senior officials, and city mayors were elected from among the senior party members and were responsible within the party for their respective realms of governance (e.g. education, health care, and economics). For example, the minister of education was also responsible for education in the ruling party; the finance minister was also responsible for finances within the party; and the mayor of a given municipality also served as its local party chairman.

The regime's presence could be detected everywhere—in every city, village, factory, and office. The country was divided into thousands of administrative units, each of which was under complete party supervision, as reflected in Figure 4.

Administrative Unit	Population Size	Representatives of the State and the Party
Prefectures [10]	Varies by prefecture	Prefect
↓	↓	↓
Subprefectures	Varies by subprefecture	Deputy prefect
↓	↓	↓
Communes or communities [145]	Approximately 30,000 residents in each commune	Commune head (*burgemeester*)
↓	↓	↓
Sectors	Approximately 5,000 residents in each sector	Commune council members
↓	↓	↓
Cells	Approximately 1,000 residents in each cell	Committee chair

Figure 4: Regime control system within the Second Republic
(numbers in brackets indicate the number of administrative units)

All prefects, deputy prefects, and commune heads were appointed directly by the president and were personally subject to his authority. In practice, the most influential officials were the commune heads, who controlled the work of government authorities in the territory under their respective jurisdiction. Citizens required the authorization of their commune head for every change of residence, for travelling from place to place, and for time spent away from home. Even selling a basket of vegetables required a permit from the commune head. In order to ensure effective supervision, citizens were required to carry their identity cards, residence permits, and authorization of employment at all times. Anyone caught without the proper documents was arrested immediately. Commune heads submitted monthly reports to the central government regarding all those who had left or entered their area of jurisdiction, so that all suspicious activity and movement could immediately be reported to the national security services.

Map 7: Administrative prefectures in Rwanda

As in the days of colonial rule, citizens were saddled with the obligation to "volunteer" workdays for public purposes. The party was in charge of coordinating the work of so-called "volunteers"—for the paving of roads, the digging of wells, and the construction of public buildings. The regime also required all academics to undergo periodic military training, apparently in order to ensure their compliance.

In accordance with totalitarian praxis, the Second Republic also instituted a cult of personality. Pictures of "the leader" were displayed in all homes, offices, and places of business. Moreover, once a week, all citizens were required to throw a party of sorts in which the "guests" were expected to sing and dance in praise of the president.

The new regime instituted not only total supervision, but total terror as well. Many members of the previous regime were murdered: President Kayibanda was starved to death in jail; journalists who displayed even the slightest critical tendencies were killed in "car accidents;" and the unemployed were assembled in special camps for "reeducation."

What historical regimes with which you are familiar bear similarity to the Habyarimana regime?

Like the Kayibanda regime before it, Habyarimana's dictatorship received the support of the Catholic Church. As part of the alliance between the state and the church, clergymen had been integrated into the institutions of the regime. For example, for many years, Catholic Archbishop Vincent Nsengiyumva, a member of the MRND central committee, conducted prayers, wearing a shirt with a photograph of President Habyarimana. The heads of the Protestant churches also typically supported the president. In practice, this "Christian Republic" was a puritanical dictatorship in which poverty-stricken neighbourhoods were demolished by order of the authorities. Drugstores that dared to sell contraceptives were also slated for destruction.

Although the regime relied to a great extent on the party and the church, in essence it was an aggressive military regime that rested on the support of the country's security forces: the army, the national police force (gendarmerie), the Presidential Guard, and special commando forces. The National Development Council (Conseil national du développement), the parliament of the Second Republic, was actually a fictitious body consisting exclusively of members of the MRND. It goes without saying that like the rule of law, elections were also fictitious (for example, in the 1983 presidential elections, the president received 98.98% of the vote). Because the regime was neopatrimonial in character,[15] purchasing its supporters with money, bribery, and jobs, it controlled all the focal points of economic power, such as the electric, gas, and bus companies, and the companies responsible for marketing agricultural produce.

The regime of the Second Republic was based on northern Hutu in its entirety. The National Development Council had almost no Tutsi members, with 2 (of 128) in 1982 and 2 (of 70) in 1990. In 1990, the government of Rwanda had only one Tutsi minister and one Tutsi prefect, and no Tutsi commune heads. Ethnic and regional quotas were set for the public administration: Tutsi could make up no more than 10% of the public administration, while a minimum of 60% of the positions were designated for northern Hutu (Mamdani 2001, 139). In practice, the regime maintained the previous government's policy. All regime officials regarded the Tutsi as "invaders" and "foreigners," and worked to ensure that they would enjoy no representation in the government, the parliament, the public administration, or the security forces. The policy of anti-Tutsi quotas remained in place within the education system and the university (see Table 5), and military men (who were all Hutu) were prohibited from marrying Tutsi women.

It is important to bear in mind that harsh discrimination was not practiced against the Tutsi alone, but also against Hutu who did not hail from the north. All senior regime officials were northern Hutu, and they took measures to ensure that all senior positions and military command positions were filled by northern Hutu from the prefectures of Gisenyi, Ruhengeri, and Byumba. Hutu from the central region of the country, and southern Hutu (Banyanduga) in

---

[15] A neopatrimonial regime is a regime of corrupt oligarchs in which no practical distinction is made between public and private funds.

particular, had no share in the regime. Almost all investments flowed to the north, with the prefectures of Kigali, Ruhengeri, Gisenyi, and Cyangugu with 90% of all investments in the 1990s, and the prefectures of Gitarama and Kibuye receiving only 1%. (Only 0.16% of the budget was invested in Gitarama, the prefecture of former President Kayibanda, and 0.84% in Kibuye). The remaining prefectures received 9% of the budget (Uvin 1997, 108). The northern regime was determined to take revenge on the Hutu from the central and southern regions of the country, who ruled the country between 1962 and 1973.

The dominant figure in the ruling oligarchy of the Second Republic was Lady Agathe Kanzinga Habyarimana, who came from a family that, until the 1920s, had controlled one of the principalities in the northwestern region of the country. Agathe Habyarimana was known for her brutality and popularly referred to as Kanjogera, the name of the mother of King Musinga, who ruled Rwanda in the nineteenth century and was infamous for her tyrannical ways. With the president hailing from Gisenyi prefecture and his wife from the Bushiru region, the two were considered to be of pure Bantu origin—a term referring to a large number of ethnic groups in Africa with common linguistic and cultural traits. They were also regarded as "purer" than other Hutu, as there was no intermarriage with Tutsi in the northern Bantu regions, where the Tutsi were reviled as colonial occupiers. It was in fact Agathe's "clan," whose members were known as "madam's clan" (le clan de Madame) or the "small house (Akazu),[16] which controlled Rwanda throughout the years of the Habyarimana regime.

Le clan de Madame included the following individuals:

- Colonel Pierre-Célestin Rwagafilita, Agathe's brother
- Protais Zigiranyirazo, Agathe's brother and a former Ruhengeri prefect
- Séraphin Rwabukumba, Agathe's brother and a Rwandan businessman

---

[16]   Akazu, or the "small house," was the term used in traditional Rwanda to refer to the inner circle of the king's court. After 1985, the term was also used to refer to the inner circle of the Habyarimana regime to indicate that this group was abusing its access to power, in part in order to acquire personal wealth.

- Elie Sagatwa, Agathe's cousin and husband of the president's sister; the president's personal secretary; and the man responsible for security in the presidential palace

- Laurent Serubga, a close associate of Agathe

- Noël Mbonabaryi, a close associate of Agathe

- Théoneste Bagosora, the president's son-in-law and director of the cabinet in the Rwandan Defence Ministry

- Félicien Kabugu, a Rwandan businessman and father of Habyarimana's daughter-in-law

- Alphonse Ntivivamunda, Habyarimana's son-in-law and a senior official in the Ministry of Public Works

---

In what ways was the Rwandan regime totalitarian, patrimonial, and oligarchic?

It should be noted that, despite its totalitarian aspects, the regime enjoyed the enthusiastic support of Belgium and France due to the fact that it represented Rwanda's "democratic majority," and because of its "commitment to Christianity," its "support of the West," and its emphasis on "development and modernization." The Christian-democratic parties in Italy and Germany also lent their support to Rwanda's "Christian-democratic" regime.

2

THE 1994 GENOCIDE

THE ROAD TO GENOCIDE (1990–1994)

In about 100 days, between early April and mid-July, 1994, some 800,000 Tutsi were murdered in what became the swiftest genocide in history.

The Opposition Parties

1990–1994 seemed to be a period of democratization and liberalization in Rwanda, motivated by the pressure of the Rwandan intelligentsia at home, donor nations and a variety of international organizations. As a sign of the change ushering in this new era, the ruling party changed its name from National Revolutionary Movement for Development (*Mouvement révolutionaire national pour le développement* or MRND) to National Republican Movement for Democracy and Development (*Mouvement républicain national pour la démocratie et le développement* or MRNDD).

In July 1990, President Habyarimana appointed a national commission to carry out reforms. One of the changes it recommended was transition from a single-party dictatorship to a multiparty system. In this context, 1991 witnessed the establishment of the following opposition parties, which from that point on were to play a pivotal role in Rwandan politics:

- The Democratic Republican Movement (*Mouvement démocratique républicain* or MDR)—heir to the ruling MDR-Parmehutu party of the First Republic. The party was headed by Faustin Twagiramungu; its members were southern Hutu, primarily from the regions of Butare and Gitarama. The party was in favor of democratization, as long as this did not include steps that might threaten Hutu domination of the country. As Hutu constituted the decisive majority of the Rwandan population, the party saw no contradiction between democratization and Hutu domination in the form of a Hutu-dominated majoritarian regime.

- The Social Democratic Party (*Parti social démocrate* or PSD). Consisting primarily of educated, urban southern Hutu, the PSD supported democracy, peaceful interethnic relations, and social-democratic social policies.

- The Liberal Party (*Parti libéral* or PL)—a mixed, predominantly Hutu, party that also represented numerous "Hutsis" (children of mixed Hutu-Tutsi marriages), including some members of the party leadership. The party was supported primarily by the educated and relatively affluent urban middle class and espoused liberal economic policies. It was led by Justin Mugenzi (who murdered his wife in 1976 and was subsequently pardoned).

- The Christian Democratic Party (*Parti démocratique chrétien* or PDC)—a Hutu party linked to the Catholic Church, and with close ties to the Christian democratic parties of Belgium, Italy, and Germany.

The Coalition for the Defence of the Republic (*Coalition pour la défense de la république* or CDR)—an extremist, racist Hutu party, to the political right of the ruling party. Its members played a major role in inciting and carrying out the 1994 genocide. Ironically, CDR founder Shyirambere Jean Barahinyura, an educated man who studied at universities in Germany and the Soviet Union, had previously been a member of the RPF (see below), but left the party after concluding that it had nothing to offer the Hutu.

In August 1991, the first four parties listed above joined together to form the opposition *Comité de concertation de l'opposition*, which they called Bloc and which could be classified as democratic and located to the political left of the ruling party.

The combined international and domestic pressure brought about a democratization process and the establishment of a national unity government, which included the MRNDD and the leftist opposition Bloc (for some reason, parties that made up this Bloc continued to be referred to as "opposition" parties even after they joined the government). Habyarimana remained on as president, but the newly appointed prime ministers—Dismas Nsengiyaremye (from April 1992 until July 1993) and Agathe Uwilingiyamana (from July 1993 until her assassination in April 1994, at the onset of the genocide)—hailed from the opposition MDR. The coalition agreement stipulated that the government would consist of nine ministers from the MRNDD and ten ministers from the opposition Bloc (three ministers each from the MDR, the PL, and the PSD, and one from the PDC). In January 1993, it was also decided to replace the single-party parliament with a temporary parliament in which the opposition was to enjoy even greater representation than they did in the national unity government.

In 1992, the ministers of the opposition Bloc, who represented the push for liberalization, exerted considerable influence on policy making in a large number of areas. Extremist prefects were fired and replaced by members of the Bloc; the minister of education terminated the use of ethnic quotas in the higher education system (and as a result was attacked by Hutu thugs); and an attempt was made to limit the activities of the national security services.

Party	Number of Representatives
MRNDD (Ruling Party) National Republican Movement for Democracy and Development	11
MDR Democratic Republican Movement	11
PL Liberal Party	11
PSD Social Democratic Party	11
PDC Christian Democratic Party	4
Other	11

Table 6: The Provisional Parliament (January 1993)

ESTABLISHMENT OF THE RWANDAN PATRIOTIC FRONT (RPF)

Concurrent with the establishment of the Hutu opposition parties and attempts to encourage liberalization in Rwanda, Tutsi began to organize themselves politically and militarily along the Ugandan-Rwandan border. With this, a new force took center stage in the country's unfolding saga: the Rwanda Patriotic Front (RPF), a largely Tutsi guerilla movement that declared war on the ruling regime. The movement was founded in Uganda, its members primarily recruited from among the community of Tutsi refugees who had fled Rwanda in the 1960s and 1970s. They were joined by members of Tutsi refugee communities from other countries, such as Burundi, Tanzania, Kenya, Cameroon, Senegal, Congo-Brazaville, Belgium, the United States, and Germany.

From the beginning of their exile, the Tutsi refugee community outside Rwanda maintained strong ties to their homeland by means of a diverse network of organizations and newspapers, sustaining their longing for "the land of milk and honey," and insisting on their right to return. Its members were persecuted and discriminated against in Uganda by the regimes of Milton Obote (1962–1971, 1980–1985) and Idi Amin (1971–1979). In the 1980s, furious with the Rwandans for their support of Uganda's opposition Democratic Party (DP), Obote's ruling party and government dismissed Tutsi refugees from their positions in the civil administration, turning a blind eye to attacks on their homes, and even beginning to expel them to Rwanda.

In response to these policies, thousands of Rwandan Tutsi joined Yoweri Museveni's National Resistance Army (NRA), which had been fighting Obote's regime since 1980. When Museveni's forces seized the Ugandan capital city of Kampala in December 1986, 4,000 of his 14,000 soldiers were Rwandan Tutsi. The most prominent were Fred Rwigyema, commander of the NRA and the first defence minister in Museveni's government, and Paul Kagame, the NRA's deputy intelligence chief. Rwigyema and Kagame had joined Museveni's Front for National Salvation (FRONASA) in Tanzania in 1973, and had taken part in the invasion of Uganda that led to the toppling of Idi Amin in 1979. Rwandan Tutsi also served as heads of the NRA training structure, the military police, and the medical corps.

By the late 1980s, the romance between the NRA and the Rwandan Tutsi had come to an end due to a variety of factors: the overall negative attitude toward Rwandans prevalent in Uganda at the time, the hostility of the Baganda (who regarded the Tutsi as economic competitors),[1] the resentment harbored by various commanders because of the Tutsi's considerable influence in the NRA, and Museveni's efforts to appease the northerners in Uganda. These factors led to the removal of General Rwigyema as commander of the NRA in 1989, an end to the promotion of Tutsi within the Ugandan army, and a return to a policy of discrimination.

In response to these developments, thousands of Tutsi left the Ugandan military, joined the Rwandan Patriotic Front (which was established in 1987), and began preparing an invasion of Rwanda based on the military skills they had acquired in the Ugandan army. Ironically, some of the founders of the RPF were Hutu exiles and opponents of the ruling regime in Rwanda: Colonel Kanyarengwe, who until 1980 had served as defence minister in Habyarimana's government, and Pasteur Bizimungu, who would serve as president of Rwanda after the RPF victory in 1994. Following the invasion of Rwanda in October 1990, the RPF grew at an unprecedented pace. A large majority of its soldiers were Tutsi, 20% of whom were university graduates.

Year	Number of Soldiers
1990	3,000
1991	5,000
1992	12,000
1994	25,000

Table 7: RPF forces, 1990–1994

---

[1]   The Baganda people are the largest and best-educated ethnic group in Uganda. For hundreds of years, they maintained the traditional kingdom of Buganda, which, although still in existence, currently does not rule Uganda.

The RPF developed a new ideology, emphasizing Tutsi-Hutu national unity and denying the existence of different ethnic groups. Blame for ethnic divisions in the country was placed on the white man, as told in the following RPF song:

> It is the white man who has caused all that, children of Rwanda. He did it in order to find a secret way to pillage us. When they [the Europeans] arrived, we were living side by side in harmony. They were unhappy that they could not find a way to divide us. They invented different origins for us, children of Rwanda: some were supposed to have come from Chad, others from Ethiopia. We were a fine tree, its parts all in accord, children of Rwanda.
>
> Some of us were banished abroad, to never come back. We were separated by this division, children of Rwanda, but we have overcome the white man's trap […] So, children of Rwanda, we are called upon to unite our strength to build Rwanda […]

The RPF message was one of democratic and progressive Rwandan national unity; the movement never reverted to the colonial racial doctrine that the country's Tutsi rulers had espoused until 1959. But despite its emphasis on Hutu-Tutsi unity in Rwanda, the RPF was a Tutsi organization in which few Hutu actually played any role. For its part, Hutu propaganda cast RPF members as tribal and feudal, and as proponents of a return to monarchical rule. Although there was in fact a conservative Tutsi right wing, it was located in Burundi, not Uganda, and did not play an important role in subsequent developments.

On October 1, 1990, the RPF invaded Rwanda. After only a few days of fighting, the RPF commander Rwigyema was killed, and replaced by Colonel Kagame. The invasion was initially contained, but the RPF nonetheless managed to conquer (or "liberate" as they saw it) part of northeastern Rwanda and launch a major offensive in April 1992. Hundreds of thousands of Hutu, who believed the government propaganda that the RPF intended to kill them, fled northeastern Rwanda for their lives. France, Belgium, and Zaire (today the Democratic Republic of Congo) sent troops to support the government. Whereas French soldiers actually took part in the fighting, the Belgian government recalled its 400-member force after only one month. The Zairian forces also withdrew, albeit without the order to do so and in direct breach of authority.

The RPF invasion did much to strengthen the racist extremists among the Hutu, who now defined all Tutsi as a fifth RPF column, of which Rwanda must be "cleansed." The RPF, they claimed, aimed to establish a "Tutsi empire," encompassing Rwanda, Burundi, and parts of Zaire and Uganda.

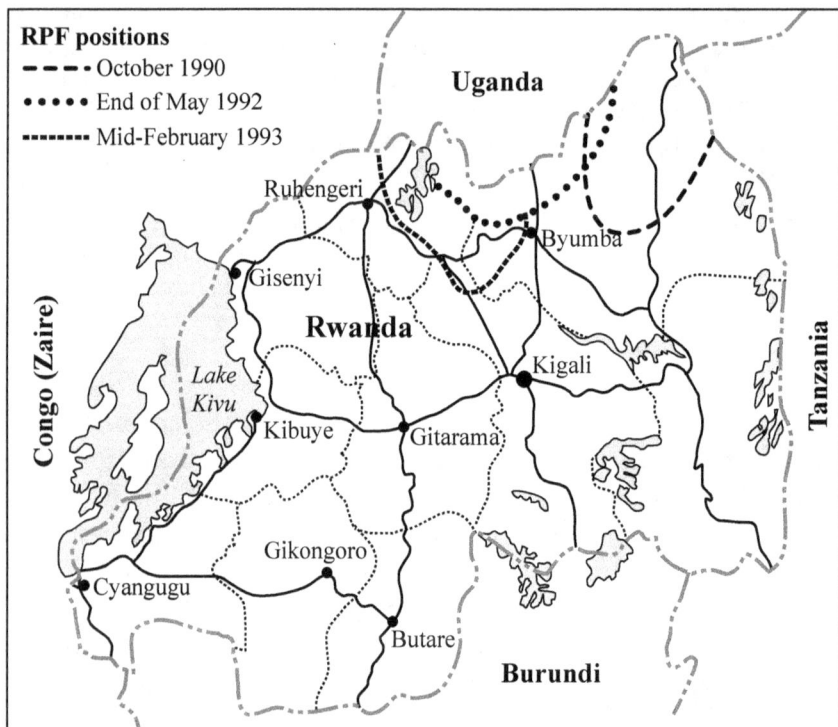

Map 8: RPF positions in Rwanda, 1990–1993

THE GOVERNMENT'S RESPONSE: REPRESSION AND ANTI-TUTSI MOB ATTACKS

The hard core of the Rwandan regime—the president, the clan de Madame (or Akazu), the ruling party, and the defence establishment—now found itself threatened by the opposition parties from within and by the RPF from without. The response was quick to come. Both Habyarimana's MRNDD and the racist CDR began establishing armed militias, for which France provided most of its weapons and training. The MRNDD set up the *Interahamwe* ("those who attack together"), and the CDR set up the *Impuzam-ugambi* ("those who have a single goal"). The government army, the *Forces armées rwandaises* (Rwandan Defence Forces or FAR), also expanded at a tremendous pace, growing from 3,000 soldiers in 1990 to 50,000 in 1994.

In an effort to gain the support of the Hutu population, the government organized massive anti-Tutsi pogroms, which left thousands dead. Such large-scale riots took place in October 1990, January and February 1991, March and August 1992, January and February 1993, and February 1994. On October 4, 1990, just a few days after the onset of the RPF offensive, the government staged an RPF attack on the capital city of Kigali and took advantage of the subsequent widespread panic to kill a great many Tutsi leaders and arrest thousands.

In the course of these developments, Tutsi inside Rwanda were not the only ones accused of being "collaborators" (*ibyitso*) with the RPF (who were again and again referred to as *inyenzi*, or cockroaches): left-wing Hutu were also suspected of working with the enemy. For example, on November 22, 1992, the MRNDD vice-chairman of the prefecture of Gisenyi described the members of the left-wing parties in the following terms:

> The opposition parties have plotted with the enemy to make the Byumba prefecture fall to the Inyenzi ... They have plotted to undermine our armed forces [...] The law is quite clear on this point. 'Any person who is guilty of acts aiming at sapping the morale of the armed forces will be condemned to death'. What are we waiting for? [...]And what about those accomplices (ibyitso) here who are sending their children to the RPF? Why are we waiting to get rid of these families? ... We have to take responsibility into our own hands and wipe out these hoodlums [...] The fatal mistake we made in 1959 was to let them [the Tutsi] get out [...] They belong in Ethiopia and we are going to find them a shortcut to get there by throwing them into the Nyabarongo River [which flows northward]. I must insist on this point. We have to act. Wipe them all out! (Prunier 1995, 171–172)

What is the ideological foundation of these words of incitement?

Following this speech, the Rwandan minister of justice, who was a member of the Liberal Party, called for the arrest of the Gisenyi prefecture party (MRNDD) deputy chairman on charges of incitement. The army, however, prevented the arrest and, instead, forced the resignation of the justice minister himself.

All this reflects the fact that by 1992–1993 the apparatus for genocide was already partly in place—bloodthirsty militias, brutal government-organized mass violence, and vicious acts of incitement.

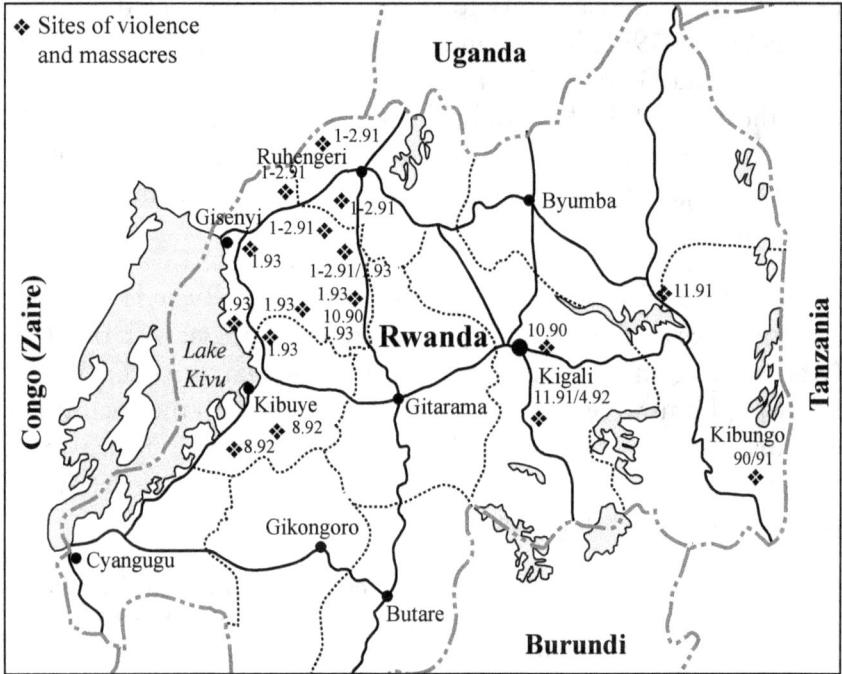

Map 9: Anti-Tutsi mass violence and massacres (1990–1993)

THE ARUSHA ACCORDS

In June 1992, under the pressure of neighboring countries (Uganda, Tanzania, Zaire, and Burundi), aid-providing nations (France, Belgium, the United States, and Germany), and international organizations (the United Nations, the Organization of African Unity, and the World Bank), a peace process between the Rwandan government and the RPF got underway. Both the Rwandan president and the MRNDD opposed the process, which was supported by the opposition leaders in the government, who conducted negotiations with the rebels. The three primary government representatives in the negotiations (all moderate Hutu) were:

- Agathe Uwilingiyamana of the MDR, who served as prime minister between July 1993 and her assassination at the onset of the genocide, on April 7, 1994.

- Defence Minister James Gasana of the MRNDD, whose dovish views made him exceptional in the ruling party and who, in August 1993, was forced to flee to Europe, for fear of his life.

- Foreign Minister Boniface Ngulinzira of the MDR, who was also killed at the onset of the genocide, on April 11, 1994.

The parties reached a series of agreements stipulating a ceasefire (July 1992): the establishment of a 19-member Broad-Based Transitional Government (BBTG) (with five ministers from the MRNDD, five from the RPF, and nine from the opposition parties—the PSD, the PL, and the MDR), to be headed by President Habyarimana; the establishment of a transitional parliament (January 1993); the withdrawal of all French forces; the return of all displaced Hutu to their homes in northern Rwanda; disciplinary action against the instigators of the anti-Tutsi mob attacks (March 1993); and a protocol for the return to Rwanda of all Tutsi refugees in Uganda (June 1993).

In August 1993, the above agreements were incorporated into the Arusha Accords, named for the town in northern Tanzania where they were signed. The agreement also included a decision to unify the government forces and the RPF into one army, in which 50% of the officers and 40% of the soldiers had to be RPF members, in order to reduce the total military force to 19,000 soldiers (at the time, government forces stood at 30,000 and RPF forces at 20,000 soldiers). The Arusha Accords also called for the dispatch of UN forces to oversee its timely implementation. At the request of the RPF, the UN forces would not include French soldiers because of France's support of Habyarimana's government.

Throughout the entire negotiation process, which lasted from June 1992 until August 1993, President Habyarimana and his associates expressed grave reservations about the peace process, repeatedly declaring that their views had not been represented at the talks. The radicals in his camp (the clan de Madame, the militias, and the

CDR) accused the opposition parties, and even some members of the ruling party, of selling out the Hutu. Under pressure from the opposition Bloc within the government, the RPF and the countries engaged in mediating between the parties, President Habyarimana was forced to sign the agreement. Though he apparently had no intention of implementing it, he, too, was nonetheless accused of defeatism by Hutu extremists.

Opposition to the Arusha Accords and Preparations for the "Final Solution"

Who will survive after the March War? [...] The masses will rise with the help of the army and the blood will flow freely!

(Excerpt of a poem[2] in Prunier 1995, 222)

The text clearly and succinctly expresses the approach of the Rwandan military to the Arusha Accords, which it thought had robbed it of its victory. Opposition to the agreement further intensified when the military provisions it contained became known. Army personnel feared they would lose their jobs (as the agreement called for a drastic reduction in the size of the joint military force) and also worried that RPF members would seize control of the military. A clandestine military group, known as AMASASU, took steps to prevent the two armies from integrating. In Kinyarwanda *amasasu* means bullets. It also stands for *Alliance des militaires agacés par les séculaires actes sournois des Unaristes*; that is, Alliance of Soldiers Annoyed by the Underhanded Secular Acts of the Unarists. The *clan de Madame* staunchly opposed the agreement, as did the overwhelming majority of the MRNDD, the CDR, and a large number of prefects and commune leaders. They feared losing their positions to members of the opposition parties and the RPF.

At the same time, dramatic developments were taking place within the opposition parties as well, as many members regarded the agreement as too far-reaching and as making too many concessions to the Tutsi. Extremist propaganda—which maintained that

---

[2]   Published in the CDR magazine Kangura in January 1994.

the RPF aimed to reinstate Tutsi rule and to oppress the Hutu in Rwanda—proved effective, as each opposition party now split into two factions: an ethno-nationalist Hutu faction opposing the Arusha Accords, and a faction that remained loyal to democracy and to the peace process. On October 23, 1993, the MRNDD, the CDR and the extremist factions of the opposition parties (in conjunction with President Habyarimana) formed an extremist bloc that opposed peace and engaged in anti-Tutsi incitement. This bloc, known as Hutu Power, was made up of:

- The MRNDD
- The CDR
- The majority of the MDR, including the Democratic Republican Youth (*Jeunesse démocrate républicaine* or JDR
- The majority of the PL
- The minority of the PSD
- The minority of the PDC
- The *Interahamwe*, the militia of the MRNDD
- The *Impuzamugambi*, the militia of the CDR

The slogans used at the founding assembly of the Hutu Power movement included calls such as Hutu Power! *Interahamwe* Power! All Hutu are One Power! Or MRNDD Power! CDR Power! MDR Power! JDR Power!

A number of senior government ministers of the opposition parties, including the prime minister and the foreign minister, did not join Hutu Power and remained loyal to the Arusha Accords. As we have seen, they paid for this with their lives when the genocide began, following the events of April 6, 1994.

The extremists were not satisfied with organizing themselves political-ically only. Thousands joined the armed militias, and large quanti-ties of weapons were distributed to the masses. One businessman with close ties to the president imported half a million machetes, and *Radio-télévision libre des mille collines* (RTLMC), an extremist CDR-run radio station, began to broadcast in August 1993. The "need" for a "final solution" to the Tutsi problem was discussed with increasing frequency.

In your opinion, how can we explain the fact that, despite the talk about genocide and the preparations then underway, the Tutsi neither appealed to outside parties for assistance nor fled for their lives?

The United Nations Assistance Mission to Rwanda (UNAMIR) started its activities in the country in November 1993. The next month, the RPF ministers, who were slated to join the provisional, broad-based government in accordance with the Arusha Accords, reached the capital city of Kigali, escorted by a battalion of rebels charged with guaranteeing their safety. The joint government was never established, however, and when the RPF ministers left the capital in January 1994, street battles erupted between supporters and opponents of the agreement.

FROM SUMMIT MEETING TO GENOCIDE

On April 6, 1994, a summit meeting of the regional leaders was held in Tanzania's capital Dar es Salaam to discuss efforts to implement the Arusha Accords. The summit was attended by the presidents of Tanzania, Uganda, Burundi, and Rwanda, and by Kenya's vice-president. The first decision taken was to establish the Broad-Based Transitional Government (BBTG). That same evening, the plane carrying Rwandan President Habyarimana and President Cyprien Ntaryamira of Burundi back to Kigali was shot down by a missile fired from somewhere near the Rwandan capital city. Both presidents and other officials (including the chief of staff of the Rwandan army) were killed instantly. The plane was downed at 8:30 pm, and within just a few hours, the *Interahamwe* set up roadblocks and began distributing lists of people that were to be assassinated. At the same time, RTLMC began broadcasting calls to avenge the death of the president. Although it is still unclear who shot down the plane, a number of interesting hypotheses were advanced:

- The operation was an initiative either of the French authorities or of a private French party. This theory is based on the fact that the missile used to shoot down the plane was French, and that François de Grossouvre, President François Mitterand's advisor on African affairs, who enjoyed close ties with President Habyarimana, allegedly committed suicide the following day.

- The attack was carried out by Belgian soldiers serving in the UN forces in the country (UNAMIR): This theory was espoused by a number of government supporters, but has no factual basis.

- Former Rwandan army officers carried out the attack as an act of revenge for having lost their jobs in 1992 after their personal failure in the war.

- The assault was initiated by Hutu opposition leaders, who regarded the removal of Habyarimana as the last opportunity for implementing the Arusha Accords. Prime Minister Agathe Uwilingiyamana was accused of involvement in the attack, although one may assume that this accusation was aimed at justifying her assassination the next morning, on April 7, 1994.

- The plane was shot down by the RPF: This was the explanation adopted by most Hutu extremists, who used it as a pretext to launch a campaign of murder and massive retaliation against the Tutsi. There were rumors of a secret report that maintained that the operation had been carried out by a clandestine RPF cell (code-named "the net") under the command of RPF commander (and, subsequently, Rwandan president) Paul Kagame. There were also reports that, on April 6, 1994, RPF forces were instructed through the media to advance toward the capital. If the RPF leadership did in fact regard the president as an obstacle to the implementation of the agreement, this theory is logical. However, it is hard to believe that they did not realize that an alternative Hutu leadership would be even more extreme.

- The plane was shot down by Hutu extremists, most likely army personnel or militiamen close to the clan de Madame.

The last hypothesis seems most likely for a number of reasons:

- Within an hour of the time the plane was shot down, the Hutu militias began their killing spree, based on previously prepared lists of people to be assassinated. It is doubtful whether they would have been able to get organized so quickly had they not known about the operation ahead of time.

- Immediately following the attack, the militias murdered the civilian population of the area in which the attack had taken place. We can assume that this was done to ensure there would be no eyewitnesses.

- The Presidential Guard prevented UN forces from reaching the scene.

- Colonel Bagosora, the extremist leader who became the architect of the genocide, and had gone on vacation on March 30, returned to the capital on April 4, just two days before the attack.

- On April 3, 1994, a RTLMC broadcast announced that "on 6 April, there will be a respite, but "a little thing" might happen."
- The March 1994 issue of the racist monthly magazine, Kangura, denounced President Habyarimana as a "collaborator" with the Tutsi.

However, if we accept this hypothesis, the question as to why the Hutu extremists killed their honored president still remains open. They apparently did so because he had yielded to international pressure, signed the Arusha Accords, and, at the summit meeting, agreed to the establishment of a transitional broad-based government. Despite Habyarimana's extremist views, Hutu hard-liners feared that he would refuse to lend a hand to the "final solution" they had planned. It is quite possible that they believed that accusing the Tutsi of the president's murder would mobilize Hutu support for the extermination of all Tutsi, and that such a seemingly "spontaneous" reaction would serve as an effective cover for what was actually a meticulously planned genocide (see also Des Forges 1999, 181–185)

Immediately following the downing of Habyarimana's plane, reserve-force colonels Théoneste Bagosora and Pierre-Célestin Rwagafilita (who were suspected of having planned the assassination) seized control of the political arena by ensuring that all moderate opposition ministers were assassinated, too, including the prime minister and foreign minister, who had supported the Arusha Accords. After failing to persuade the army to seize control of the government, the two colonels established a Committee of Public Safety (*Comité de salut public*), which appointed an all-Hutu Power government, consisting of the MRNDD, the MDR, the PL, the PSD, and the PDC. Former National Development Council president, Theodore Sindikubwabo of the MRNDD, a pediatrician, was installed as president, and Jean Kambanda of the MDR's Hutu Power faction was appointed prime minister. The most influential actor behind the scenes, however, remained Colonel Bagosora.

For unknown reasons, the UN and the international community granted diplomatic recognition to the new, radically racist government, which immediately began implementing its murderous policies. The commander of the army and a few of the more moderate prefects, who refused to take part in the "final solution," were removed to ensure that the security apparatus and the government be able to work unhindered toward fulfilling the "vision." RTLMC broadcasts left no room for doubt regarding the nature of this vision. Over and over, broadcasts encouraged the killing, with calls such as "you have missed some of the enemies in this or that place. Some are still alive," and "the graves are not yet quite full. Who is going to do the good work and help us fill them completely?"

Hutu Tutsi Rwanda Burundi

In the land of our ancestors
where Lucy[3] roamed
where now we send our guns
and our guilty planes of useless food
In a place where we stuff
our thoughts and feelings
so we can paint someone else
so very black
Can you see the soldier boys
running in the streets?
Can you hear the children crying?
Do you know the dead and dying all about?
In this shadow world is also grace and beauty
In this shadow land is a distant cry to be free
In this darkest night is the warmth of a fire long forgotten
Cradle of civilization
of man and womankind
(Osbourne, 2000)

---

[3] Lucy was the name given to the oldest human skeleton ever found in Africa.

Illustration 3: "Men Killing Friends." (Drawn by a child who survived the genocide.)

THE PERPETRATORS

Who were the killers in Ntarama? Units of the Presidential Guard came from Kigali. The Interahamwe were brought in from neighboring communes. Youth who had been trained in self-defense units after the civil war began provided the local trained force. But the truth is that everybody participated, at least all men. And not only men, women, too: cheering their men, participating in auxiliary roles, like the second line in a street-to-street battle.

When we captured Kigali, we thought we would face criminals in the state; instead, we faced a criminal population.

If the violence from below could not have spread without cultivation and direction from above, it is equally true that the conspiracy of the tiny fragment of génocidaires could not have succeeded had it not found resonance from below.

(An RPF commander in Mamdani 2001, 6–7)

Genocidal killing is never sporadic—it is always organized by the state, the government, and the ruling authorities. And so it was in Rwanda. The killing was not perpetrated by a wild mob that had lost control. Rather, the campaign was well planned, well organized, implemented in an efficient, systematic manner, and orchestrated by political, military, administrative, economic, and intellectual elites. Amongst the most prominent proponents, planners, and organizers of the genocide were:

- Prof. Ferdinand Nahimana, a historian who directed the RTLMC's broadcasting campaign of incitement

- Colonel Theoneste Bagosora, the director of the Rwandan Defence Ministry Cabinet and the most powerful figure on the scene after April 6, 1994

- General Augustin Bizimana, who was appointed defence minister after April 6, 1994 and immediately urged the army to join in the massacre

- Major Aloys Ntabakuze, commander of the Rwandan military's Para-Commando Battalion
- Major Protais Mpiranya, commander of the Presidential Guard Battalion
- Joseph Nzirorera, secretary general of the MRNDD
- Jean-Bosco Barayagwiza, leader of the CDR and commander of the *Impuzamugambi*
- Robert Kajuga, president of the *Interahamwe*
- George Rutaganda, vice-president of the *Interahamwe*
- Félicien Kabuga, Rwandan businessman and bankroller of RTLMC and the *Interahamwe*
- Pascal Musabe, Rwandan banker and a commander of the *Interahamwe*
- Members of the clan de Madame or the clan des beaux-frères (Agathe Habyarimana and her brothers)

Although only a few dozen members of the elite had planned the genocide, these key individuals controlled organizations with tens of thousands of members. The institutional and organizational network that formed the extermination apparatus was directed by the following groups:

- The militias of the MRNDD and the CDR (the *Interahamwe* and the *Impuzamugambi*, respectively)
- The Presidential Guard, which consisted solely of northern Hutu
- The Rwandan Gendarmerie (regional police)
- The Rwandan Armed Forces (FAR), which consisted of 40,000 soldiers, did not take part in the genocide from the outset, but joined in the killing on April 8, 1994, when the RPF resumed fighting
- Government bureaucrats—prefects, subprefects, commune heads, and local council members—as well as the apparatuses at their disposal.

However, not all extremist Hutu leaders affiliated with Hutu Power were in agreement with the "final solution." Despite the fact that President Habyarimana belonged to the extremist faction of the Hutu, he was apparently unwilling to support the genocide. We can assume that his murder on April 6, 1994 aimed to clear the way for a progenocide leadership.

Although the genocide was organized from above, its leaders succeeded in mobilizing the country's farmers, the undernourished, and the unemployed. In contrast to other genocides, such as the Holocaust and the Armenian genocide, the genocide in Rwanda was ultimately a case of one people murdering another people. A significant number of Hutu actively participated in the genocide. Indeed, in 2001, the number of suspected murderers still being held in Rwandan jails stood at 130,000. In addition to the Rwandan Hutu, tens of thousands of Hutu refugees from Burundi also took an active role in the killings in Rwanda, as an act of revenge against their country's own Tutsi regime.

As we now know, Hutu churches and priests also took part in the killing. Moreover, on April 10, 1994, when the killing was at its height, the bishops, who had been affiliated with the Hutu state for many years, declared their support for the new government. Not only did they fail to condemn the killings, but they actually called upon their flocks to follow the government's instructions. This provided the genocide with religious and moral legitimacy in the eyes of the politicians, the bureaucrats, the propagandists, the officers, and the rank-and-file murderers. Some church officials even volunteered to help the government, and explain its policy to the European countries, the United States, and the United Nations. On August 2, 1994, twenty-eight Catholic priests wrote a letter to the Pope, categorically denying that an act of genocide had taken place. As we have seen, many priests betrayed religious Tutsi who had sought refuge in churches, and others even participated actively in the killing. The Protestant churches behaved similarly. Only a handful of lower-level priests actually opposed the atrocities, a decision for which they sometimes paid with their lives.

The middle strata of killers also included a large number of doctors and teachers. Astonishingly, human rights activists took part in the killing as well. For example, Innocent Mazimpaka—chairman of the Rwandan League for the Promotion and Defence of Human Rights (*Ligue rwandaise pour la promotion et la défense des droits de l'homme* or LIPRODHOR)—was involved, along with his brother, in the murder of Tutsi in the town of Gatare. Of the commune's 12,263 Tutsi, only 21 survived.

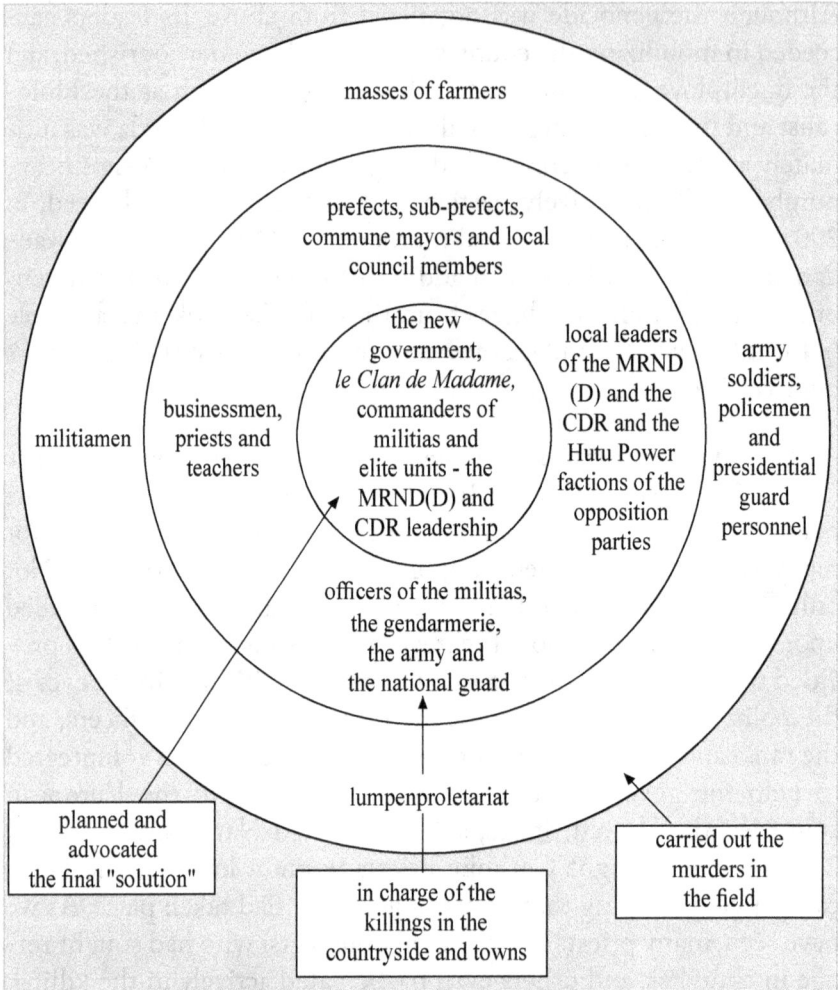

Figure 5: Hierarchy of the perpetrators of genocide

The murderers were not all motivated by the same concerns. Many in the leadership acted out of a strongly held belief in a racist ideology, maintaining that a "final solution" to the "Tutsi problem" was a necessity. Many others were driven by their personal hatred for the Tutsi. Greed also played an important role in mobilizing both the elite and the masses. The killing offered the elite a way to acquire Tutsi homes, cars, computers, and other property. The farmers, on the other hand, were guaranteed the agricultural crops, livestock, and furniture of their Tutsi neighbors. As for the hungry proletariat, a bit of food and alcohol was all it took to entice them. The open sanctioning of looting was hence an important means of mobilizing the general public, and the looting itself was carried out with the approval of the authorities. Some were also motivated by fear of the RPF and by official propaganda, spreading stories about the "discovery" of Tutsi plans to kill Hutu and steal their property. Others were induced to take part in the killing by the directives of the civil authorities, including mayors, police chiefs, party leaders, teachers, and local priests. And as always, many, attracted by a mob mentality, joined in the killing.

Consider whether the motivations listed above were similar to the factors that motivated perpetrators of other genocides.

THE VICTIMS

Our enemy is one
We know him
It is the Tutsi.

(Hutu song in Des Forges 1999, 203)

The genocide was carried out in two phases. During the first phase (April 6–11, 1994), the killing was selective and resulted in tens of thousands of deaths, mostly from among the Tutsi elite, but including a small number of Hutu as well. The second phase (April 12–July 15) was pure genocide, resulting in the deaths of hundreds of thousands of Tutsi.

In the first phase, moderate Hutu were executed to ensure that they would not serve as obstacles to the "final solution." Among them were Prime Minister Agathe Uwilingiyamana (along with her entire family), Foreign Minister Boniface Ngulinzira, Landwald Ndasingwa, leader of the democratic faction of the PL, and Joseph Kavarunganda, president of the Rwandan Constitutional Court. Faustin Twagiramungu managed to escape before the murderers reached his home. At the same time, thousands of Hutu intellectuals, journalists, human rights activists, lawyers, and priests associated with the opposition were also murdered, in accordance with lists that had been drawn up long before April 6. For example, in Butare, the killers murdered almost all the professors and students of the National University of Rwanda, which included mainly moderate Hutu, and a smaller number of Tutsi. Most of the Hutu killed were from the southern and the central regions of the country, and associated with the democratic factions of the MDR, the PL, the PSD, and the PDC. Thousands of Tutsi were also killed, including leaders, academics, well-to-do Tutsi, and people known to support the RPF.

Now that preparations for the second phase were completed, the "final solution to the Tutsi problem" began. During this phase, an estimated 800,000 Tutsi were killed (85% of the Tutsi in the country, which accounted for 12% of the population of Rwanda). Women, children, and babies were killed on the premise that women needed to be killed because they would eventually bear children, and children needed to be killed because they would grow up to be adult Tutsi. RTLMC broadcasts repeatedly called on listeners not to repeat the "mistake" of the 1960s, when Tutsi children were permitted to leave the country, only to return in the 1990s as commanders of the RPF. Most of the Tutsi were "small Tutsi" (petits Tutsi)—poor villagers whose lifestyle, unlike that of the Tutsi in the towns, was actually more similar to that of the Hutu. Other Tutsi victims were men with Hutu wives (since in such marriages, the father was believed to determine the ethnicity of the children) and Tutsi women with Hutu husbands (in some cases, the Hutu men killed their own wives). Sometimes, Hutu men were murdered as a punitive measure for marrying a Tutsi woman. The children of mixed marriages were also killed—children of Tutsi fathers because of their Tutsi ethnicity, and children of Tutsi mothers in order to ensure that they would not avenge their mothers' murder in the future. The Hutu song quoted at the beginning of this subchapter provides a good indication of the general atmosphere during the critical days of the genocide.

It was not always easy to identify Tutsi, as they lived in the same villages and the same neighborhoods as the Hutu. Identification was usually based on characteristic Tutsi physical traits, such as tall and slim body shape, a long straight nose, long fingers, and thin lips. Nevertheless, in some cases Hutu were murdered based on misidentification: their murderers mistook them for Tutsi, even though they could have examined commune records or identity cards, which indicated the holder's ethnicity. Some people informed on their neighbors, making the murderers' work "easier." Militiamen who knew how to distinguish between Hutu and Tutsi also patrolled the villages and the city streets. The task of distinguishing between Hutu and Tutsi was especially easy in cities, where identification was sometimes based on dress alone. For example, well-dressed people were typically identified as Tutsi and shot.

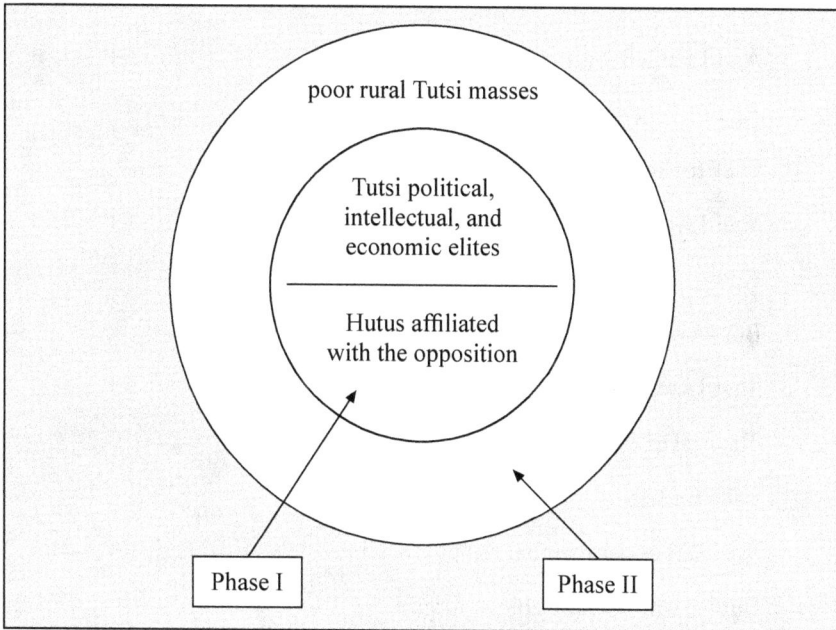

Figure 6: General breakdown of the victims of the two phases of the genocide

Why? [4]

Why did you die as if you loved no one?

Why did you die as if no one loved you?

What have they made of you?

What have they made of us?

You never harmed a soul,

You shared so much love.

And I am left with oceans of tears.

All of a sudden, everything changed,

They took you and left me, and later I grew.

Your love is always here, but it is so far away.

All its oceans have dried up.

But when I again envision the day

That I saw your face for the last time,

The oceans roll back to me.

Then we left,

We tried to put together the pieces,

But we will never be able to forgive.

In the eyes of god, everything can be forgiven, I am certain.

But how can we wipe away the hatred that refuses to disappear?

How can we forget what shattered our lives?

I think about it every day, everyday I suffer.

Father! Oh how I wish you could see me growing up.

Why? Why? Why?

(Marie-Yolanda Ujeneza Ngulinzira in Ngulinzira 2001, 60)

---

[4]   The poem "Pourquoi" was translated form the French into Hebrew by Edo Abarbaya.

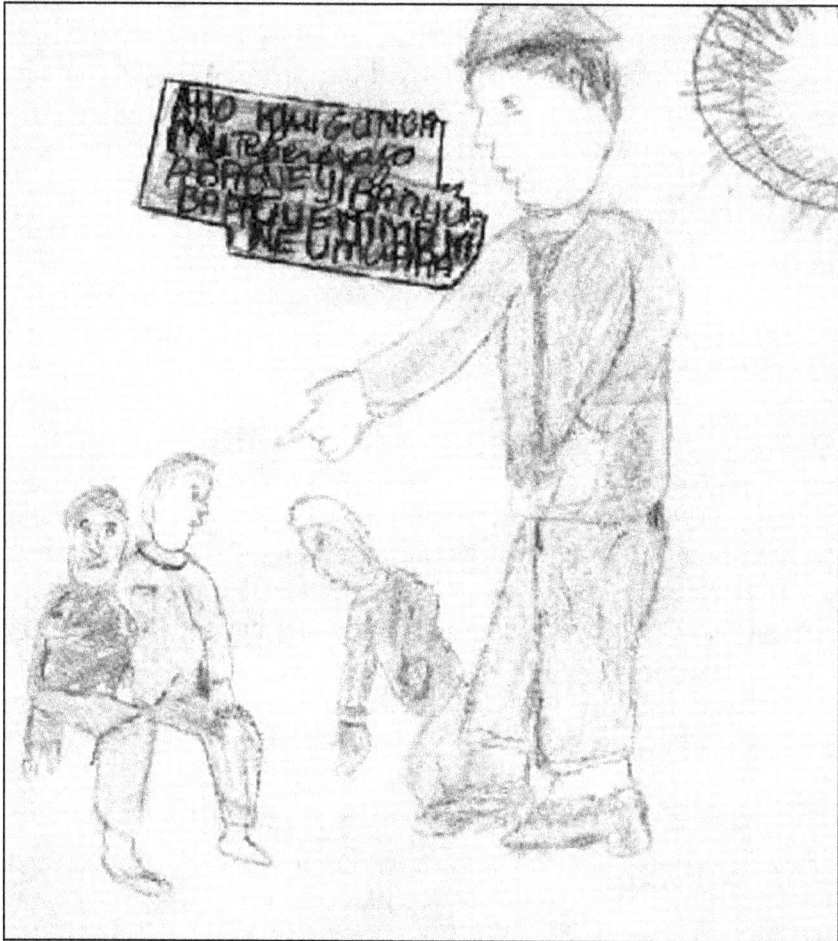

Illustration 4: "Don't think about the death of your parents. Come on, let's play soccer." (Drawn by a child who survived the genocide.)

THE METHOD

Like all genocides, the genocide in Rwanda was planned ahead of time and systematically implemented. It was not a spontaneous, unavoidable outburst of primordial savage violence, and Rwanda was not a "failed state" that had crumbled or deteriorated into anarchy. On the contrary, the totalitarian Rwandan regime was ubiquitous, and had thoroughly prepared its representatives for the "final solution." A military planning team labored over detailed plans for the extermination of the "racial enemy." It is also known that, at least in the first phase of the genocide, the authorities were provided with orderly lists of individuals earmarked for extermination. It is difficult to understand why the Tutsi did not sense what was happening. All in all, this attests to the efficiency of the planning and the high level of secrecy maintained.

The killing apparatus operated in an organized and hierarchical manner. Orders were issued from above; from the government to the army, the militias, and the gendarmerie; from command headquarters to units in the field; from the government to prefects; from prefects to subprefects and commune mayors; and from subprefects and commune heads— by means of popular meetings—to the general public. Every echelon exerted constant pressure on the one below, just as did the radio broadcasts, which played a crucial role in the creation of an appropriate climate for mass murder.

Structure of the Killing Apparatus

As we have noted above, Rwandan communities typically accepted the citizens' duty to obey the authorities when they were mobilized for public works, or *umugand*. This usually included the paving of roads, digging of wells, construction of public buildings, and other such projects. Local government officials took advantage of this traditional practice to mobilize the people for the killings. They summoned Hutu to meetings that included inflammatory speeches emphasizing the obligation to kill the "cockroaches" and "collaborators." The meetings also involved ceremonies of song and dance, promises that looted property—from beer bottles to cattle—would be distributed to the murderers, and threats against all those who failed to take part in the undertaking.

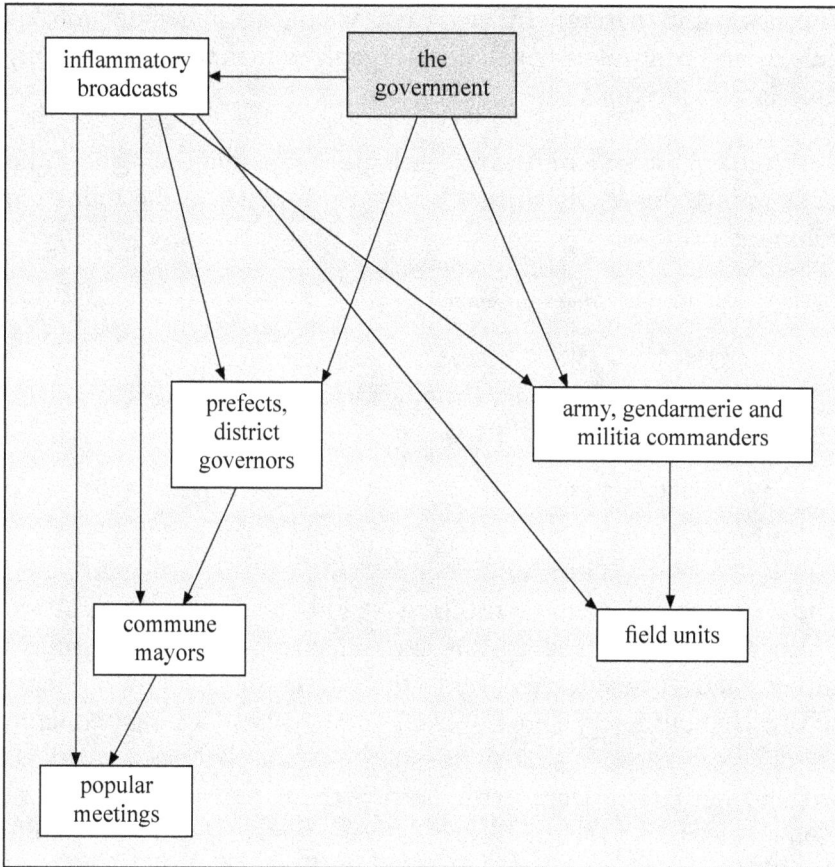

Figure 7: Structure of the killing machine

The authorities took care of all aspects of organization, such as herding the victims into schools, hospitals, churches, and other public buildings; the transportation of victims to where they were to be slaughtered; the distribution of weapons and looted property, and the disposal of bodies in hidden mass graves.

International humanitarian studies' scholar Peter Uvin maintains that the mass mobilization for genocide in Rwanda was effective because the order to kill was issued from above. This relieved the murderers of any moral dilemmas by dehumanizing the victims—who were referred to as "cockroaches," "feudalists," and "murderers"—and by portraying the killing as a routine act. The complex killing machine helped the general public view the killing as commonplace and natural. In any case, whenever genocide unfolds quickly and continuously, and in an organized manner, there is rarely time to ask questions (Uvin 1998).

In summary, the system that so efficiently facilitated the work of the killing apparatus in Rwanda was based primarily on the following components:

- Dehumanization of the enemy
- Inflammatory radio broadcasts
- An ordered succession of commands issued from above
- Mass mobilization
- Guaranteed rewards
- Intimidation

The system was vicious and ruthless. Neighbors murdered neighbors. Store owners murdered customers, and vice-versa. Hutu teachers turned their Tutsi students over to the militias or killed them themselves. The murderers were not even deterred from killing people in churches or in hospitals. Tutsi priests, doctors, and nurses were killed without hesitation, along with Tutsi patients and wounded. Hutu women married to Tutsi husbands were forced to kill their children, because they were considered to be Tutsi. Many Tutsi women were raped before being killed, and the bodies of victims were often defiled in horrifying ways. As we have noted, Hutu who refused to take part in the killing were also murdered.

During the killings, official Rwandan propaganda painted a distorted and wholly false picture of the events. The propagandists speaking on the radio and at public meetings portrayed the Hutu as victims acting out of self-defense. Tutsi, in contrast, were depicted as subversives who were plotting to kill Hutu, and the RPF was portrayed as planning to reestablish the Tutsi kingdom, feudalism, and slavery. All the Hutu were doing, they maintained, was frustrating a Tutsi conspiracy to turn the clock back to the period before the "social revolution." The systematic killing of Tutsi was portrayed as a product of the "spontaneous anger" of the masses, who were mourning their beloved slain president. The events were not even referred to as murders, but rather as "war" and "battles," in order to convince the Hutu themselves that they were fighting in self-defense, and to conceal from the world what was actually going on in Rwanda.

In your opinion, how was the genocide fueled by precolonial and colonial traditions?

The Media

> *The grave is only half full. Who will help us fill it? We will not repeat the mistake of 1959. The children must be killed too. By 5 May, the country must be completely cleansed of Tutsis.*
>
> (Excerpt from an RTLMC broadcast[5] in Destexhe 1995, viii, 32)

As we have seen, the media in general, and radio broadcasts in particular, played a pivotal role in the genocide. Most homes in Rwanda had a radio and virtually the entire population heard radio broadcasts. Until April 1993, Radio Rwanda, with its periodic anti-Tutsi incitement, was the only radio station in the country. In March 1992, the station spread the rumor that the Tutsi were planning to kill Hutu leaders in the city of Bugesera. As a result, the *Interahamwe* instigated anti-Tutsi mass violence in which 300 Tutsi were killed. In April 1992, the opposition assumed control over the official radio station, which subsequently ceased to serve as a mouthpiece for Hutu extremists. As a result, the racist radio station RTLMC, dubbed "radio death" by Rwandan genocide survivors, was established in April 1993. This station played a major role in the service of the genocide.

The RTLMC, often dubbed "the Hate Radio," (Martin 2002, 24) was run by members of the Rwandan establishment. The station's steering committee included the son- and brother-in-law of President Habyarimana, government ministers, the governor of the National Bank of Rwanda, the secretary general of the MRNDD, representatives of the CDR, and *Interahamwe*'s vice-president. The

---

5   In April 1994.

editor in chief was also editor of the MRNDD magazine, and most journalists were affiliated with the CDR. Key personnel at the radio station included history professor Ferdinand Nahimana, mentioned above, and linguistics professor Léon Mugesera. All the equipment used by the station was owned by the government, which provided it with different frequencies.

RTLMC broadcasts were in Kinyarwanda (unlike Radio Rwanda, which broadcast in French) and were casual and light in genre, including popular music, slang, and crude jokes. As a result, masses of Rwandans eagerly tuned in. The contents of the broadcasts were brutally racist, portraying Tutsi as domineering foreigners, traitors, thieves, and murderers, and accusing them of taking control of Rwanda's wealth, education system, churches, and aid organizations. They were also charged with aspiring to reestablish the "Nilo-Ethiopian feudal dictatorship." The station repeatedly urged listeners to kill, uproot, and "cleanse" the country of its Tutsi enemy. It also broadcasted lists of names of opposition members to be assassinated, and directed the public to their places of hiding.

In the course of the genocide, RTLMC developed its own glossary of terms, which included chilling metaphors and euphemisms for the killing that was underway:

- "A big job" = genocide
- "Tree felling" = killing
- "Hurricane" = genocide
- "Bush clearing" = chopping up men
- "Pulling out the roots of the bad weeds" = slaughtering women and children (Hintjens 1999, 268–269; Prunier 1995, 142).

The press also played a role in preparing the ground for genocide. With a 50% literacy rate, Rwanda was a relatively educated African country. Most daily newspapers, weeklies, and monthly magazines were affiliated with the racist Hutu establishment. The anti-Tutsi content of the monthly magazine Kangura was particularly vicious: It began inciting readers against the "cockroaches" as early as October 1990, and was known for its hate-inspiring caricatures. The article excerpt presented below, which appeared in March 1993, is typical of Kangura content and style:

We began by saying that a cockroach cannot give birth to a butterfly. It is true. A cockroach gives birth to another cockroach . . . The history of Rwanda shows us clearly that a Tutsi stays always exactly the same, that he has never changed. The malice, the evil are just as we knew them in the history of our country. We are not wrong in saying that a cockroach gives birth to another cockroach. Who could tell the difference between the Inyenzi who attacked in October 1990 and those of the 1960s. They are all linked . . . their evilness is the same. The unspeakable crimes of the Inyenzi of today [...] recall those of their elders: killing, pillaging, raping girls and women, etc. (Des Forges 1999, 73–74).

In December 1990, Kangura published the "Hutu Ten Commandments," (for a more detailed discussion of this document, see chapter 5) which articulated the following main principles:

- Every Hutu male should know that Tutsi women, wherever they may be, are working in the pay of their Tutsi ethnic group. Consequently, shall be deemed a traitor: any Hutu male who married a Tutsi woman; any Hutu male who keeps a Tutsi concubine; any Hutu male who makes a Tutsi woman his secretary or protégée

- Strategic positions in the political, administrative, economic, military and security domain should, to a large extent, be entrusted to Hutus

- Hutus must cease having pity for the Tutsi.

Never before in the history of genocide had the media played as important a role as it did in the genocide in Rwanda. Radio broadcasts and print journalism clearly conveyed to the public the message that the "big job" was being done with the approval of the authorities. The incitement from above, transmitted through all the communications media, systematically prepared the ground for the "final solution." It is safe to assume that without the media as a catalyst, the hatred from below would not have resulted in genocide, certainly not on such a scale.

To the best of your knowledge, how did the media's role in the Rwandan genocide differ from the media's role in other genocides? What was the unique significance of the use of the media in this case?

EVIDENCE FROM THE
SCENE OF THE MURDER[6]

Massacre at Kansi

In the commune of Nyaruhengeri also, local leaders decided that April 18 was the time to begin large-scale killing. Until that day, Hutu and Tutsi had worked together at roadblocks and on patrols. Near the church of Kansi, Tutsi teachers had at first been afraid to take their places at the barrier and did so only after Hutu had promised that they would not harm them. Thousands of people had sought shelter in the church and adjacent buildings after the burgo-master, Charles Kabeza, had refused to let displaced persons come to the communal offices. Saying he had been ordered not to allow them to gather at the offices, he had put a barrier in place to keep them at a distance. The parish priests had sought without success to get the Red Cross to provide food for the displaced, who were also lacking water.

In the afternoon of April 18, retired soldiers or military men in civilian dress came to goad Hutu into attacking Tutsi at the barrier near the church. At first the Hutu hesitated, but then they began to throw stones at the Tutsi, who threw stones back. That night, armed men attacked the church complex and killed some Tutsi. The next morning workers warned the priests, who had spent the night in the rafters of the church, that a major attack would come that night. The priests, who had not been able to get even food for the displaced despaired of getting any protection for them. They advised the crowd to flee, but leaders of the group asked "Flee to where?" Many were already weakened by lack of food and water. Unable to save the thousands of people, one of the priests gave them absolution and left. As he passed behind the church, he was caught by an assailant who put his machete to the priest's neck and warned him

---

[6]   This entire section consists of excerpts from Alison Des Forges' *Leave None to Tell the Story*. They are based on interviews conducted by a Human Rights Watch team with murderers, survivors, and bystanders. See Des Forges 1999, 452–454, 472–487, 497–494.

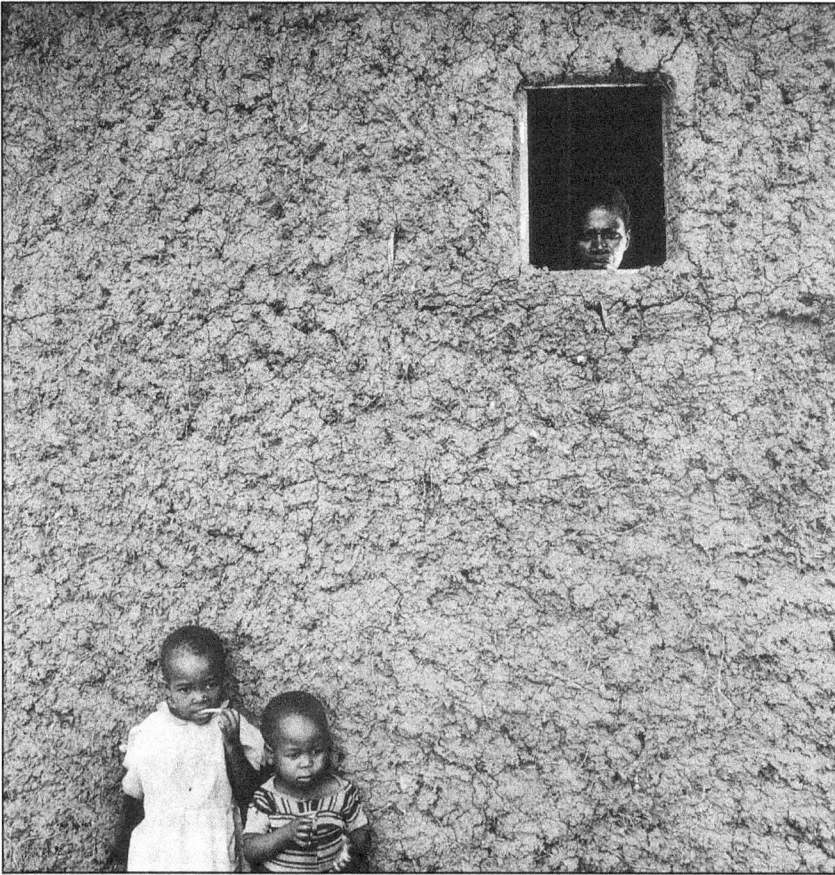

Illustration 5: "My children are frightened of death"

My baby was three months old. I ran away with him and we hid in the hills. His older sister is now 14 years old. Then, I thought she was dead. They beat them in the head with machetes and left them there. No one here sleeps peacefully at night. When it rains, I think they are pelting my house with stones, and I stand alone at the entrance keeping watch. Those nights are long. If only the sun could never set (Tasiana, age 48).

to stay clear of the killing that was going to take place.

That afternoon assailants killed the director of the school outside the convent of the Bernadine sisters. Shortly after, former soldiers and communal councilors led thousands of armed men in attacking the church and school buildings, beginning with grenades and finishing with machetes. In a few hours of intense slaughter, they killed between 10,000 and 10,500 persons. During the attack leaders used plastic whistles to direct the activities of the killers. Among the killers were Burundian refugees who had been housed at the Nyange camp not far from the church.

The next day, one of the priests found ten or fifteen survivors outside the main door of the church. As he stood talking with them, he heard assailants blowing their whistles in the same rhythm that they had used the day before. From the woods behind him, a crowd surged forward and killed the survivors before his eyes. When the priest later entered the classrooms, the killers once more came after him and killed babies who had survived the massacre of the day before. When he asked them why they were murdering infants, they replied, "They are the enemy."

For the next six days, local people were too occupied with searching for survivors and plundering to help dispose of the bodies. Dogs came to eat some of them. After the six days, the burgomaster sent men to help with the burial. The church paid for the labor.

Pillagers made off with everything portable from the church and school buildings, even items for which they had no possible use. When the burgomaster appealed for the return of some of the goods, people did bring them back. Some who regretted having killed asked the clergy, "Will God punish us?"

The Hutu at the barrier who had promised the Tutsi teachers that they would not harm them kept their promise. Burundian refugees killed them instead.

On April 18, the same day as the massacres at Simbi and Kansi, administrative officials and political leaders launched the slaughter of between 2,000 and 3,000 people who had taken refuge at the communal offices in the commune of Kigembe, just south of Nyaruhengeri. On the same day, assailants spread out over the hills of the commune Huye, burning and killing in all sectors except Mpare. And in the northeast, assailants from outside the prefecture and others from the commune of Muyira drove Tutsi, including those displaced from further north, from Muyira into Ntyazo, just to the south.

In your opinion, should the massacre described above be classified as organized mob attacks or as spontaneous attacks?

Systematic Slaughter in Towns

Killing the Targeted Individuals

As in Kigali, soldiers—particularly Presidential Guards, members of Nizeyimana's bodyguard, and troops from Ngoma camp—along with National Police began the slaughter by targeting people from the intellectual and political elite of Butare. They went directly to the homes of those selected ahead of time for slaughter, sometimes relying on local guides or asking directions from neighbors. Militia backed up the members of the regular armed forces. In addition to the dozens of *Interahamwe* who had apparently been discreetly brought in during the previous ten days, one hundred or so Presidential Guards and militia arrived in Butare on April 20. An AC-130 transport plane landed at Butare airport between 4 and 5 p.m., perhaps the first time such a large craft had used the small landing strip. Struck by the arrival of such an unusual plane and by the appearance of unknown soldiers and militia in town that evening, many people assumed that the strangers had been flown into Butare. In fact, they had arrived by bus while the plane, flown by Belgian pilots, had come from Nairobi to evacuate a group of European nuns and UN military observers. In addition to militia from outside Butare, local killers reportedly led by Shalom Ntahobari, also began the most damaging of their attacks on April 20.

Although soldiers and militia killed some people in their homes, they took many to be executed at one or another of the main killing grounds, like that behind the museum or in the arboretum of the university or near the psychiatric center and the Groupe Scolaire. Beginning late in the day of April 20 and continuing for the next three days, residents of Butare town reported hearing frequent bursts of gunfire, particularly from these execution grounds.

The soldiers began the slaughter in the pleasant neighborhood of Buye, striking leading Tutsi such as Professor Karenzi. Presidential Guards from the group that protected Habyarimana's brother, Dr. Bararengana, came for Karenzi at about 2 p.m. on April 21 and took him to the barrier manned by soldiers of the ESO in front of the Hotel Faucon. There he was lined up with a number of other people, including another professor who was accused of having falsified his identity card. According to a witness, a militia member from out of town then killed two men, two women, and five children under the eyes of Prefect Nsabimana and Vice-Rector Nshimyumuremyi who stood a short distance down the street, in front of the Hotel Ibis. One of the other men bolted and ran for his life and Professor Karenzi was shot and killed immediately afterwards. Soldiers returned shortly after to the Karenzi home and murdered the professor's wife. The children and young people of the household were hidden in the ceiling and escaped, although all except one would later be killed too.

When killing began in Cyarwa, witnesses immediately recognized that it was being done systematically. One man first heard shots behind his house at about 1 p.m., then others from a house next door. He stated:

> The soldiers who came had very clear objectives: Ndakaza was a supporter of the PL, a Tutsi, who lived in the house behind mine; Sinzi Tharcissse, who was at the national university; Simpunga who worked at the Butare Economat and who was a member of the PSD; and Gregoire Hategekimana, an administrator from the university, who was a member of the MDR. The soldiers went down the street behind me and then up my street and stopped at these particular houses.

Another witness to the same events not only heard the perpetrators, but saw them clearly from his enclosure. He declared:

> The trouble began in Cyarwa on the afternoon of the 21st. We heard gunfire first from the direction of Rango. People coming from the market said that soldiers had shot a man named Venuste and then had gone to his home and had killed everyone there. The soldiers then proceeded down the

line, killing as they went. I could hear the sound of gunfire, moving in a line around my house, since the street behind follows a wide arc that circles back towards my house.

A few of those killed were officially Hutu on their identity cards, but someone had done research and had learned that they had previously been Tutsi. Someone had gone to the home communes of those who were suspected to check on whether they were really Hutu or Tutsi:

> I saw the deputy [Laurent] Baravuga leading three or four soldiers who were carrying South African rifles [probably R-4 rifles]. He had a list. He knew the area well and could direct them. The soldiers were Presidential Guards and they were followed by a large crowd of people. After the soldiers had finished and moved on, the crowd would move in and loot the house. I saw people streaming by carrying refrigerators, radios, anything. Nearly everyone from Cyarwa joined the crowd and they were happy to steal.

During the first days of attacks, a crowd of militia and others in Cyarwa found that not all Tutsi were to be considered targets. They forced their way into a large building where several women friends of interim President Sindikubwabo had taken refuge with their families. The assailants were rounding up the Tutsi and preparing to kill them when Presidential Guards from Sindikubwabo's house hurried to the scene and ordered them to leave. The assailants did not want to give up their intended victims, but the Presidential Guards threatened them with grenades and made them withdraw.

In addition to political and intellectual leaders, the military targeted the rich. In the heart of Butare, soldiers invaded the home of a prosperous businessman on April 20 and extorted some 300,000 Rwandan francs (about US $1,700) as the price of his own life and that of his family. Two days later, a young soldier named Claude came back with three *Interahamwe*, reportedly from the group headed by Shalom. They took five young adults and a twelve-year-old boy with them and walked the short distance to the killing field at the Groupe Scolaire where they murdered them.

In Tumba six National Policemen led a crowd in attacking the home of a Swiss entrepreneur who had a Tutsi wife. The ordinary people were armed with machetes, spears, and even a bow and arrow—wielded by a young man wearing a baseball cap with the visor behind, in the fashion of foreign young people. The National Policemen fired a couple of warning shots and forced their way in. After having robbed the family of several hundred thousand Rwandan francs, they called in the civilians, who looted the house. Some of the crowd stole valuable items, but others seemed almost embarrassed at what they were doing and took items of little or no value, like a cooking pot full of potatoes or a child's toy. To one observer, they seemed to be participating because they had no choice. They left without injuring anyone.

Soldiers killed important Hutu who were thought to oppose the genocide, just as other troops had killed Hutu officials of the national government in Kigali. According to witnesses, Nizeyimana and soldiers of his guard murdered his neighbor, Deputy Prosecutor Matabaro. Soldiers also slew the professor Jean-Marie Vianney Maniraho, who had criticized the heavy military presence in town at a public security meeting, and his family.

In Cyarwa, soldiers burned down the home of a Hutu woman related to a national leader of the MDR who opposed Hutu Power. Several days later, she was killed at a barrier, reportedly on the order of Deputy Baravuga. Soldiers and militia killed the sub-prefect Zéphanie Nyilinkwaya and fourteen others of his family during the night of April 21. A Hutu member of the PSD, Nyilinkwaya was seen as a potential leader of resistance to the slaughter of Tutsi. A MSF doctor came by Nyilinkwaya's house early on the morning of April 22 and found the corpses of the family scattered over the drive in front of the house. Among them was a child three months old, shot in the back of the head, lying at his mother's breast, which had also been blown open by a bullet. The doctor found two survivors, a girl about seventeen years old, who had been shot by a bullet that had passed through both breasts, and a fourteen-year-old boy. When he prepared to take them to the hospital, two soldiers came at the run to stop him.

Killing by Neighbourhood

While most soldiers concentrated on the elite targets, others, together with National Police supervised the militia that swept through neighborhoods eliminating Tutsi. A frail resident of the working-class neighborhood of Ngoma, in her mid-eighties, observed the genocide with horror. She had seen the killing of Tutsi since the 1950s but, she said, this slaughter was different because "it killed babies on the back, children who were beginning to walk, pregnant women, old people." She declared:

> The militia always came escorted by soldiers, two or three of them. The soldiers did not kill, they just accompanied the militia and watched them kill. They came many times over many days: attack, leave, attack, leave. They came during the night, attacking one family, then leaving. Then they came the next night and attacked another family. Maybe three families in this place in one night. Then, tomorrow, five families over there.

During the day, there were rumors about who would be attacked that night. They had meetings in town to plan. Sometimes, they said, "Tonight we will attack a family with this number of people in the household, this number of children." Those listening tried to guess which family was being talked about. Children especially would move about, listening, and come to give warnings. Children and household workers moved between houses, between houses and the meetings, between houses and the bush. Sometimes they would get paid for going to listen. But there were other children, too, who spied on those who were giving warning.

While some were in meetings others were out on the streets, moving around, poking around, trying to find the people who were hiding inside houses. Those who did the spying included women, prostitutes, and girls who did not have husbands.

Illustration 6: "It all remains engraved on my heart"

In 1959, my husband forged the information on his identity card. People came to us and told us that they would not kill us. But they returned a few months later. The children fled, but my husband and I stayed. They killed them with axes. They thought of Tutsi as snakes. Most of my neighbors are in prison. Their families don't even give me water. I must forgive, even if I am angry. What can an old woman like me do? I will never forget. It all remains engraved on my heart. It is better it keep it inside. God will judge them (Marie, age 66).

The old lady lived in a well-built house at the corner of two streets. One street runs along the ridge on which most of Ngoma sits; the other cuts across the first and descends steeply into the valley which separates Ngoma from the rest of the town of Butare. Starting on the night of April 21, she saw the crowds surging down the street, some of them dressed in banana leaves, and always with their military escort:

> I hid and saw it from the window, from behind the curtain, cowering there in the corner. I saw them driving the groups of people ahead of them, shouting and shoving them with sticks and wooden clubs. Behind them came the soldiers with their guns, but they did not shoot. I saw a pregnant woman get hit in the stomach and fall back. I heard her cries. They took them down to the valley and killed them with nail-studded clubs, with hoes and machetes. I heard no shots, only the cries of horror and pain from the valley.

The elderly woman, herself a Hutu, became a target when informers told the militia that she was hiding her Tutsi grandchildren. Knowing that sheltering Tutsi put her own life at risk, the elderly woman also took in one teenaged girl who was not part of her family but who had fled to her home in the middle of the night. While the witness was peeking out from behind her curtain, she saw the girl run, bent over, into the enclosure that surrounded the house. She opened the door and the girl threw herself inside and collapsed unconscious on the floor. When the girl revived, she recounted how the rest of her family had been slain or fled to an unknown destination. The old woman allowed her to stay with the young people of her family. They hid in the bush during the night and came in furtively during the day to get something to eat.

The militia who came three times to search this home included people from the neighborhood and those from the adjacent sector of Matyazo. The two groups, which joined together outside her front door, were supervised by two soldiers. Most came on foot, but they also had a couple of vehicles to transport whatever they were able to pillage from this house or others they intended to attack that night.

At the time of the second search, Shalom Ntahobari led the group. He particularly wanted to find the girl whose midnight arrival had been noticed by local informers. He knew her older sisters well and had often dined and spent the evening at the girl's home. Shalom and his followers forced their way into the house and demanded to know where the girl and the others were hiding. He had a machete stuck in his belt. When the old woman said there was no one there, he grabbed her by her two ears and twisted them to try to make her talk. She said nothing. They searched the house thoroughly, but found no one. Two days later, they returned, again ready to kill. Once more they had to leave empty-handed and angry. Soon after, someone came to rescue the old woman and her charges. As they drove away, she saw the crowd arriving for another search.

The witness remarked that many who invaded her house were strangers, but, she added, "Even the ones I knew, I couldn't recognize them. They had transformed themselves into animals. They were like lions." Another witness in Ngoma remembered what he saw outside his window:

> I saw people out on the street, carrying clubs, axes, and machetes. They were all wearing MRND or CDR hats. Those without hats wore banana leaves around their necks or over their shoulders. They wore portrait pins of President Habyarimana on their chests. Even the youngest also tried to carry a weapon or a stick and were wearing the portrait pin. Even the young members of the PSD were wearing the hats of the CDR and the MRND and the portrait pin. We could not understand how that was possible because the PSD was opposed to the MRND and the CDR.

After the first attacks on April 20, assailants moved on to other neighborhoods in the following days. In Cyarwa, soldiers and militia herded the crowd of Tutsi down the street in the middle of the day and beat them to death at a bridge, at a place known as Gateme. In one part of Tumba, the physician Munyemana reportedly organized the patrols and supervised the arrest and detention of Tutsi who were locked in the sector office, to which he had a key. In another part of the sector, the cell leader and employees of the university laboratory guided National Police to the homes of Tutsi. In both Cyarwa and Tumba, Hutu and Tutsi had collaborated until April 20 in protecting their sectors from outsiders, so some Tutsi joined the patrols organized on April 21, believing they were still part of the defense, not the enemy. They were killed by their fellow patrol members. In the sector of Sahera, assailants attacked the home of Aristarque Rwigimba, who was able to hold them off with the help of a stout door and a bow and arrow. But the assailants returned the next day with a communal policeman, who shot two of the resisters, making it possible for the assailants to kill nine others in the house.

At Kabutare, teachers and staff members from the Groupe Scolaire secondary school lived in a tight-knit community just down the road from the school buildings. Of the sixty-five or seventy families in one neighborhood, five wereTutsi or mixed Tutsi-Hutu households. Soldiers, reportedly guided by the cell leader, Faustin Twagirayezu, arrived one morning and went directly to the houses where Tutsi lived. They were followed by a gang of street kids who tagged along after the soldiers to watch the violence. According to one of the community who was present that morning,

> We stood in front of our houses, unable to do anything at all. We waited, knowing what had happened elsewhere, waiting our turn to have it happen here, waiting with our arms folded.

The soldiers took several Tutsi men, one Tutsi woman, and a Hutu and headed down towards the psychiatric center. According to one witness, they chose people at random from the onlookers and tried to get them to beat the Tutsi to death, but those selected refused to do the job. The soldiers locked the captives in the local canteen, saying they were too hungry to kill at the moment. They went away, telling local people to guard them. In the opinion of one onlooker, that measure was not necessary because they would not have tried to flee anyway. Later that day, the soldiers returned with civilians from outside the community. They beat the captives to death. A witness who heard the soldiers coming a second time called his children to come in the house, not wanting them to see what would happen. He went outside himself, pretending to read a notice that was posted on a tree. He saw the soldiers go into the house of a neighbor named Joseph and then went back inside his own home and closed the door. All those taken away were killed and their families were killed three or four days later. The witness added, "That finished our neighborhood and they never came back."

Once the killing campaign was launched, soldiers and militia acted as though they had license to kill anyone who looked Tutsi. On April 23, a Zairean couple, Mr. Kisasa Lukasa and his wife, were traveling through Butare and stopped at the market. While Mr. Lukasa went to make some purchases, his wife stayed in the car. Militia or soldiers passing by the vehicle noticed her and asked for her identity papers. When she could not produce them immediately, they killed her on the spot.

Clarify for yourselves the forces and the groups who carried out the murders.

Slaughter at the University and the Hospital

While some soldiers and militia were targeting neighborhoods in town, others began killing at the university. Classes were in recess for the Easter vacation, but some students had stayed in residence to prepare for examinations and others fled to the university once killing began elsewhere because they hoped to be safe there. Beginning on April 8, soldiers had restricted movement to or from the campus and authorities had prepared a list of students in residence, supposedly to facilitate their passing the soldiers' barrier. Students, already polarized by previous events such as the February killings, formed into two groups, that of Hutu Power and that of Tutsi and those willing to support them. The Hutu Power students, known as the LIDER group from the name of their student association, began playing the music of anti-Tutsi singer Bikindi and staying up at night to see what the others were doing. The Tutsi students and others of their group also organized into four teams of guards who took turns keeping watch at night. They moved to rooms other than those where they usually slept and the LIDER students tried to keep track of where they were.

At mid-day April 21, soldiers killed a student at the campus barrier and another either at the barrier or in town. That evening, they came to round up Tutsi students as they entered the cafeteria, checking them off on a list as they were taken. A few Tutsi students saw the roundup beginning and managed to flee along with Hutu friends. The soldiers took those captured either to the arboretum adjacent to the campus or across the road to a woods on the grounds of the national research institute. LIDER students then took up the search for those students not yet found by the soldiers. As they discovered Tutsi who had hidden in the rooms, under the beds, or elsewhere, they took them out to deliver to the soldiers. One student was found at about 3 a.m. by a group of fellow students who kicked and beat her before taking her and another student across the road to the soldiers in the woods. As the student recalled,

> The soldiers there said that these were the last students they would take. They said not to bring any more to them, because they were finished for the day. The two soldiers took us and pushed us into the woods. They cocked their guns and I thought it was all over. But then they spoke to us. They asked us if we would have anywhere to hide if they let us go. I said I had an aunt in Cyarwa and Aimable had a cousin in town. And so the soldiers told us to run. They fired their guns into the air so that the students would think that we had been killed and they left.

Aimable and I went further into the woods. It was full of cadavers. There were bodies everywhere, many, many of them. There was nowhere else we could go, so we had to stay there until it got light, there among the bodies.

The next morning, the two students sought refuge at the nearby university hospital, which was still quiet. One of the two was eventually killed, but the second survived.

According to the vice-rector, some 650 students were at the university on April 20 with more arriving all the time. On May 31, there were 212 students on campus, 190 of them Rwandan, the rest from Burundi. Some students had fled, but the great majority had been killed. In a later exhumation of a mass grave near the university, some 600 bodies were found. Most of these victims were students—a significant part of the national intellectual elite in training at the university.

During the night of April 22, after students had come to seek shelter at the hospital, soldiers of the ESO and the Presidential Guard came and killed some forty Tutsi patients. One remarked to MSF staff who worked there, "The hospital stinks with Tutsi and we must clean it up." The next morning, the soldiers continued removing patients from the wards and even from the operating rooms. They also took away hospital personnel because their names were on the list of those to be killed. One of the nurses taken and beaten to death behind the hospital was a Hutu who had been caring for wounded

FAR soldiers. She was seven months pregnant with a baby fathered by a Tutsi. Over a two day period, the soldiers killed between 140 and 170 people at the hospital. After meeting authorities at the prefectural offices on April 23 to protest the killings, the head of the MSF mission, Dr. Zachariah, returned to the hospital. He later recalled:

> I looked around me with my team and people were just being taken out in groups of threes, fives, going behind the hospital. We could hear the screams. I told my team, "We are getting out of here! There is nothing more to do.

Like the university students, others had sought refuge at the hospital in late April, some of them occupying tents in the courtyard that had once housed refugees from Burundi, others hidden in the wards, closets or kitchen of the conglomerate of rambling buildings. In the days following the first killings at the hospital, soldiers returned repeatedly to search out those in hiding. One evening they took a law student named Épiphanie who was pretending to be one of the hospital staff. By this time, authorities had proclaimed an end to the killings (see below) and had said that anyone who was threatened should call for help, so Épiphanie screamed repeatedly. But no one came to her rescue and the soldiers took her away to the woods below the hospital. There they raped and beat her. A military doctor named Rwanyonga heard of the attack and went to find her in the woods. He brought her back and put her in the intensive care ward for treatment. At about 11:30 p.m., four soldiers returned and took her away and killed her.

Some of the Tutsi who had taken refuge at the hospital were from the commune of Huye. Soon after the soldiers killed the patients and medical staff, militia from that commune came, with an escort of soldiers, to collect the men and boys from Huye. The militia forced them to set out for Huye and reportedly killed them, either en route home or shortly after arriving there. According to testimony, the burgomaster of Ngoma helped pressure the Huye people to leave and allegedly also returned several times in the next two weeks, twice in the company of soldiers, to see that other Tutsi be put out of the hospital. Some of those expelled were reportedly killed at a barrier just a short distance down the road from the hospital.

Dr. Alphonse Karemera, dean of the medical school, produced an attempted justification for "cleaning up" the hospital in an official plan dated April 24—while the slaughter was still going on. Entitled "Socio-hygenic and Humanitarian Action for Victims and Persons Displaced by the War: A Proposal of the Faculty of Medicine concerning the functioning of the UH *[University Hospital]* in this period of provoked catastrophe," it was forwarded by Vice-Rector Nshimyumuremyi with his approval to the prefect. The plan called for removing refugees, displaced persons, and those not critically ill from the hospital and the tents on the hospital grounds. Those persons who, in the words of the vice-rector, "clutter up the UH without good reason" were to be handed over to humanitarian organizations and the administration. In the proposal, Dr. Karemera complained of the "suffocating lack of support personnel." Without remarking on the reason for this sudden loss of staff, he merely asked for authorization to begin recruitment for provisional replacements. He also insisted on immediate action to remedy the critical hygenic and sanitary situation in the region, that is, to remove the bodies which could become a hazard to health. Noting that the post of medical supervisor was empty for the moment, he offered the help of the faculty of medicine in supervising this work. It was apparently Dr. Eugène Rwamucyo, a member of the medical staff known for his virulent anti-Tutsi attitude (see below) who undertook this task.

On May 2, Prefect Nsabimana informed the vice-rector that the prefectural security council agreed with the proposed plan. He noted that the administration was looking for ways to take care of the remaining refugees and displaced persons still at the hospital. That same day, the director of the hospital told those who had sought shelter at the hospital to go to the prefecture; he even provided transportation to take some there. One witness who was present remembers being told that they were to go to the prefecture to get the documents necessary to go home. According to another witness:

> Then they said that everyone who was at the hospital had to go to the prefecture. The burgomasters wanted them to go back to their homes and the burgomasters were going to come fetch their people and take them back to their hills.

One of the two university students who had been captured and then allowed to escape was among those sent to the prefecture. She reported:

> At the prefecture, the *Interahamwe* were waiting. They had been told that we were coming and there were *Interahamwe* from each of the communes waiting to take their own people to kill. Our students were there too. When we arrived, we were surrounded by *Interahamwe*, they encircled us. A soldier tapped me on the shoulder and asked if I was a student from the university. I said that I was. He asked if I was alone, and I said that no, I was with another student. He asked us to follow him. He took us to the brigade. There was a crowd of people there, and they beat us. After they were done, they told us to leave. We went outside, and when we went out, another soldier tapped me on the shoulder. He asked if I knew him and I said no. And he asked if I knew what this was, and he handed me my identity card. He said that he was the soldier who was supposed to have killed me but let me go [...] He said that he would help me and so he escorted me to Cyarwa. I really do not know why.

Not all those from the hospital were taken back to their communes at this time. Some joined the group of Tutsi already at the prefecture and remained there for another two weeks.

Collective Slaughter

Butare Town

In Butare prefecture, as elsewhere, the largest numbers of Tutsi were killed in the shortest time in massacres at churches, public buildings, and other gathering places. In the town of Butare, however, the worst massacres took hundreds rather than thousands of lives because officials had not permitted massive assemblages of Tutsi within town limits.

In the first two weeks of April, several hundred Tutsi had assembled in the broad space before the prefectural offices. On April 19, as described above, soldiers removed the men from that group and apparently took them to be executed. Those left behind, mostly women and children, formed the nucleus of a group whose presence would trouble authorities until the end of June. They were shifted from place to place and dozens of them were seized at night, but they were never openly attacked in town.

Authorities had transferred six to seven hundred children from an orphanage in Kigali to the Groupe Scholaire and also had allowed several hundred other displaced persons from Kigali to take shelter in the school buildings and courtyard. On April 21, soldiers and *Interahamwe*, some of whom were wearing the distinctive green and yellow patterned tunic of the militia, came to the Groupe Scolaire as the orphans and displaced persons were eating their noon meal. They called them out to the courtyard, separated them into two groups on the basis of their identity cards, and began killing the Tutsi, mostly with machetes and clubs. Local residents, reportedly under the direction of the cell head Faustin Twagirayezu and including especially Burundians, also joined in the slaughter. According to one witness, several women, both Rwandan and Burundian, killed other women and children.

Some people from Kigali and elsewhere, at least several hundred of them, had dispersed quietly throughout the town with family or friends. Small numbers of them, like locally resident Tutsi, sought protection clandestinely in convents and other church facilities. Larger groups took refuge openly at the Ngoma church and the Rwandan Episcopal Church (*Église épiscopale au Rwanda*).

Ngoma Commune: Matyazo and Kabakobwa Massacres

Not permitted to congregate in massive numbers inside town, the displaced did assemble in the thousands at Matyazo and Kabakobwa, two sites just outside of town but within Ngoma commune. Authorities had first tried to send displaced persons gathered at Matyazo to churches at Karama and Simbi, as mentioned above, but when this failed, Burgomaster [mayor] Kanyabashi had installed them at the Matyazo health center and had arranged for police to be posted there as guards. As with such groups elsewhere, the displaced at first had freedom of movement, to go out and buy food, for example. After April 19, those inside were no longer permitted to leave. On April 21, soldiers touched off the attack on the health center by firing grenades into the enclosure and then shooting some of the people inside. Militia and local people followed up with machetes and clubs, killing most of the two to three thousand persons who had sought refuge there. A witness on a hill facing Matyazo could hear clearly the sounds of the massacre. He remembered:

> I heard all the noise from Matyazo, the explosions of grenades, preceded by
> the shouts of the young who yelled "Power," the blasts on the whistles and
> the beating of the drums. It went on until 5 a.m.

Children and infants who survived the Matyazo massacre were left
alone among the bodies for three days. Then some women came
to take the little girls home, probably to raise them as servants.
On April 25, the councilor of the sector, Athanase Nshimiyimana,
and the communal policeman, Marc Polepole, drove a truckload of
injured children to the hospital at the Groupe Scolaire. When they
attempted to transport a second group of sixty-two injured children, the soldiers at Ngoma camp said it was forbidden to transport
Inyenzi and refused to allow them past their barrier. They left the
children, who ranged in age from a few months to four years old at
Ngoma parish, not far from the barrier, where some four hundred
other people had already taken refuge. The priests at Ngoma tried to
get the Red Cross to come to take the children to the hospital, but
they also replied that it was no use because the children would just
be killed en route. A nurse, Domitilla Mukabaziga, who was among
those who had taken shelter at the church, cared for the wounded
children despite the lack of supplies and equipment. Mukabaziga
was the sister-in-law of Burgomaster Kanyabashi and called him
repeatedly during these days to ask him to rescue her, her children
and her nephew. He reportedly answered that there was nothing
that he could do for them.

The second major massacre of Ngoma commune was launched the
same day as that at Matyazo, but at the opposite end of the commune. Matyazo lies at the northern most point of Ngoma while Kabakobwa, a gently sloping site where three valleys merge, lies between
the two southernmost sectors, Nkubi and Sahera. Many Tutsi from
Gikongoro and such Butare communes as Huye, Gishamvu, and
Ngoma, some with their few heads of cattle, camped in the open
space there while deciding whether or not to continue their flight
some ten miles further to the Burundi border. From Kabakobwa,
they could have gone directly south, following the Migina River, or
they could have taken one of the two roads paralleling the river that
led to the frontier. As the slaughter intensified, more Tutsi came to
Kabakobwa, some of them told by authorities or advised by Hutu
neighbors to go there. A mile or so north of Kabakobwa was the

Rango market, one of the two markets functioning to serve Butare town and the immediate region. Thursday April 21, was a market day. Some men in civilian dress arrived at the market in late morning by bicycle and began checking identity cards among the crowds trading there. The story quickly circulated that the men were soldiers, even that they were Presidential Guards. Either these men or others in uniform shot a Tutsi named Venuste at the market. Many people then fled from the market to Kabakobwa, swelling the number of persons there. According to some estimates, there may have been as many as 10,000 Tutsi at the site.

That afternoon local people attacked the Tutsi, apparently with some support from the communal police, including at least one former soldier. At first the Tutsi repelled the attack. Some Tutsi, numbering perhaps 500, decided to flee Rwanda and headed southeast for the frontier in Kibayi commune. Most were killed before they could cross the river that forms the boundary between Rwanda and Burundi. The next morning, April 22, the communal police arrived in a Ngoma commune pickup truck and took away several Tutsi selected from the crowd. They returned later that day with soldiers and National Police who used rocket-propelled grenade launchers and machine guns to slaughter the Tutsi. That night, on the hills of Nyaruhengeri, on the other side of the valley, some local people celebrated the massacre with feasting, singing, and dancing.

The Massacres of April 30

The people at Ngoma church had only two days to enjoy the promise of safety. At 10 p.m. on April 29, militia and local crowds attacked the church buildings. One of the people inside reached the bell tower and sounded the bell for thirty-five minutes, alerting the entire region to the attack that was violating the promised peace. One of the priests called the Ngoma military camp, less than a mile distant. The soldier who answered inquired what kind of weapons the assailants carried and then told the priest, "Don't worry. They won't hurt you." Hardly reassured, the priest called the public prosecutor, Mathias Bushishi, a man from Ruhengeri who was thought to have influence with the local leaders of the genocide. Bushishi agreed to call the camp commander. Two hours later eight soldiers appeared, led by a lieutenant named Niyonteze. The officer directed his ire at the priests for sheltering such a large number of people in the vicinity of a military camp and showed no interest in arresting their attackers. He counted the number of displaced persons at the church and then he left. The assailants, kept at bay by a hail of stones from the roof, also left for the night.

The next morning, at about 10 a.m., twenty-two soldiers returned under the command of Lt. Ildephonse Hategekimana, head of the Ngoma camp. After telling the displaced people that they would be not be killed but would be taken to prison, he called in the civilians to do the killing. A witness who was hidden heard the children crying and the women begging. He heard the "dull blows, followed by small cries" which he supposed were the sounds of children being clubbed to death. Then, after an hour, silence. There had been 476 people in the church, 302 of them children. Some victims were taken off to be killed in the nearby woods, a number of the women raped first. According to witnesses, the communal policeman Marc Polepole particularly sought out the sister-in-law of the burgomaster and her children and delivered them to killers outside the church.

It rained in the late morning, but when the rain ended in the early afternoon, killers came to finish off the wounded children who were still alive, lying on the grass. As they were clubbing them to death, a vehicle belonging to the Ministry of Health appeared and several officials got out. The killers chatted with them while continuing to club the children on the ground. After the officials left, the killers pillaged the remaining rice stocks of the church as payment for their "work."

Some soldiers had searched especially for the parish priest, Abbé Jerome Masinzo, and reportedly intended to torture him before killing him, but two others helped him to hide just before the attack. One returned later and demanded 500,000 Rwandan francs ($2,800 USD) to keep the secret of the priest's location. Without any such sum available, Abbé Masinzo appealed to other church contacts who managed to obtain 50,000 Rwandan francs from Burgomaster Kanyabashi. This was the first of a number of payments delivered to soldiers as the price of the priest's life. The burgomaster agreed to help Abbé Masinzo although he was said to have refused to save members of his own family who were killed in the Ngoma massacre. On several subsequent occasions, he reportedly refused aide to other relatives, including to two little girls, one aged seven, the other aged eight. He supposedly believed that help to relatives would be more quickly discovered than aid to others and would expose him to immediate reprisals.

Apparently just after having launched the operation at Ngoma church, Lieutenant Hategekimana led another large group of soldiers, professional people from Buye, and others in searching the convent of a Rwandan religious order, the Benebikira. They brought a warrant signed by Lieutenant Colonel Muvunyi. Hategekimana ordered his soldiers and the professional people to round up everyone inside the extensive complex. Meanwhile a larger crowd of civilians stayed outside, moving around the wall of the compound, shouting and yelling.

Among the Tutsi particularly sought by the soldiers were the children and young people from the household of Professor Karenzi, who ranged in age from a seven-year-old girl to a young woman of twenty-two. After Karenzi and his wife had been killed on April 21, the young people had hidden at first in a deserted house and then had been stopped by soldiers as they tried to move to another hiding place. After looking at their identity cards, the soldiers remarked "You are Inyenzi, Tutsi" and threatened to kill them. Several soldiers were unwilling to kill, complaining that they had already killed so many people that day. One claimed to have killed eight women, another to have killed thirteen girls. A Presidential Guard appeared and insisted that the young people be taken to the police brigade. At a barrier, soldiers instructed them to sit down and pray because they were about to die. In the end, the soldiers decided to be satisfied with money and, perhaps, with raping one or more of the girls. The soldiers accused one of the girls of having rebuffed the advances of soldiers before the genocide had begun. Finally the soldiers delivered them to the convent, where they had asked to go and where they remained until April 30.

When the search party located "the Inkotanyi from Karenzi's house" at the convent on April 30, they loaded them and others into the back of a pickup truck. The soldiers climbed in to stand on top of the children. In all, they took away twenty-five people, five of them men, the others women and children. The youngest was a little girl named Aimée, who was five years old. Just as soldiers had said that the people at Ngoma church would be taken to prison and not to be killed, so the assailants said that this group was being taken to the prefectural offices for protection. When the soldiers returned later in the afternoon to loot some beer that they had noticed during the search, the sisters asked what had happened to the young people. One answered, "That's not our job. We left that to the *Interahamwe*."

An hour or so after the convent of the Benebekira was invaded, ten soldiers and thirty militia and other civilians demanded entry to the Junior Seminary at Karubanda, a short distance away. When asked why they had come, one of the group answered, "Even the clergy and the nuns have been found hiding arms for the RPF, so they can't be trusted [...] watch out if you hate our country" (AUTHOR DATE, PAGE). The search party checked the identity papers of those present and found two Tutsi employees, who were handed over to the militia. The *Interahamwe* took them to a nearby woods and beat them to death, then climbed on their bus to go home. At about 5 p.m., the soldiers returned to loot the seminary. They took a couple of the young women who were there caring for orphans as umusanzu, a "contribution" to the army. They raped them. Shortly after other soldiers came for the same purpose.

Beginning on April 20, increasing numbers of soldiers wounded in war were transported to Butare to be treated in the hospital and to convalesce in the buildings of the Groupe Scolaire. On May 1, some of these soldiers slaughtered twenty-one children and thirteen Red Cross workers whom they believed to be Tutsi. They selected them from among the survivors of the April 21 massacre and those who had taken shelter at the Groupe Scolaire since that date. The brutal killing, reported in the foreign press, drew sharp international criticism and, probably as a consequence, a reprimand from the general staff.

In light of what you have just read, do you think the killings were planned, organized and systematic, or were they spontaneous and random?

Illustration 7: "He saw his parents being slaughtered; he has no words to describe his feelings." (Drawn by a boy who survived the genocide.)

For additional testimony, see Appendix 2, which contains excerpts from a book by Yolande Mukagasana, a Rwandan Tutsi author who survived the killing, and stories by Boubacar Boris Diop, a Senegalese author whose life and thinking revolved around the Rwandan genocide.

Rwanda (Death Children)

A black monster flew over my land last night
from its belly fell a dark angel of might
I was the only survivor to see the angel from the sky
yesterday I survived a massacre and I do not know why
sitting with my dead mother not knowing if I were dead
hearing distant victory cries of the murderers of dread
I cradled my mother in my arms tilting her head to see
that's when the angel glided into the tallest tree
it must be the supernatural or evil that watches me
[I wandered aimlessly towards the edge of the trees]
I had to face this evil to save the souls of my land
I touched the forest where I first noticed evils hand
evil must be gone for I no longer sense it in the air
time passed as my mind drifted to a sanctuary of care
gurgling sounds kept drifting in and out of my good ear
I had to wake for this may be my death or evil I fear
I opened my eyes to devour images that could not be real
trees were marked with dead rebels who came to steal
rebel victory cries would never be heard again […].
(Doug Snedden, 1992)

3

THE INTERNATIONAL DIMENSION OF THE GENOCIDE

No government had any intention of stepping in to stop the Rwandan holocaust.

(Boutros Boutros-Ghali[1] in Martin 2002, 23)

The Americans were interested in saving money, the Belgians were interested in saving face, and the French were interested in saving their ally, the genocidal government.

(Alison Des Forges in Khadiagala 2002, 490)

Just as with the Jewish and Armenian genocides, the world stood idly by and watched as the genocide in Rwanda unfolded. The Tutsi were abandoned by everyone, except by a handful of volunteers from *Médecins sans frontières* (MSF) and a few other humanitarian aid groups. The writing had been on the wall: between 1990 and 1994 Rwanda had implemented a racist policy and organized periodic mob violence against Tutsi. Yet, it continued to receive economic and military aid from abroad.

By late 1993, foreign embassies in Kigali, the governments of the West, the UN forces in Rwanda, and the UN leadership in New York were all aware that preparations for genocide were underway. Despite the chilling public speeches of Rwandan leaders, the radio broadcasts, the reports from within Rwanda from Tutsi and Hutu alike, and the unconcealed arms shipments to the militias, the world failed to take action and forestall the onset of mass killing.

---

[1] UN Secretary-General.

This chapter analyzes the behavior of the major international actors in the drama that unfolded in Rwanda: France, Belgium, the United States, the United Nations, and the countries of Africa.

FRENCH POLICY ON THE GENOCIDE

You cannot deal with Africa [...] without getting your hands dirty.

(Bruno Delaye[2] in Des Forges 1999, 658)

Our mandate [the Foreign Ministry] does not authorize us to arrest them on our own authority. Such a task could undermine our neutrality, the best guarantee of our effectiveness.

(Bruno Delaye in Des Forges 1999, 686)

What pressure? There was no pressure.

(A senior French official[3] in Des Forges 1999, 660)

Improve your image.

(General Jean-Pierre Huchon[4] in Prunier 1999)

I've had enough of being cheered by murderers.

(A French soldier in Rwanda in Des Forges 1999, 681)

France's deep involvement in Rwanda began three days after the invasion of Rwanda by the Rwandan Patriotic Front (RPF) on October 1, 1990. Immediately following the invasion, France dispatched a military force (numbering between 600 and 1,100 troops at any given time) in support of President Habyarimana. The force was charged with training the Rwandan army and the presidential guard, providing tactical and strategic advice to the

---

[2]   Advisor to President François Mitterand on African Affairs.

[3]   The response of the official to the question of whether France exerted pressure on the Rwandan government to change its policies.

[4]   Advice given to leaders of the genocide by General Huchon, French military official responsible for military aid to Rwanda.

Rwandan General Staff, establishing and operating communications and artillery installations, piloting helicopters, manning checkpoints, defending the capital, and interrogating prisoners. The delegation was led by President Mitterand's military advisor.

The official assignment of the French force was to protect the French citizens in Rwanda. In reality, however, its task was to help the Rwandan government defeat the RPF. Indeed, French forces played an important role in holding back the rebels between 1991 and 1993. France also violated the UN arms embargo by supplying weapons to the Rwandan government and is known to have trained the *Interahamwe*, the brutal militia of the MRNDD.

Although France's official position on Rwanda was to support the peace process, each agreement was actually followed by increased French military aid to the racist government. Some maintain that the French regarded diplomatic and military involvement as integrated tools, to be employed in coordination with one another, while others hold that the French administration was split on the matter, with the French foreign ministry in favor of a political solution and the French defence establishment calling for a military solution. According to the French ambassador to Rwanda at the time, the reports of mob violence that periodically rocked the country between 1990 and 1994 were only "rumors." Later, in 1998, French officers testified before a commission of inquiry of the French National Assembly that, even during those early years, they had heard that the Rwandan military spoke frequently of a "final solution."

The bulk of the French force withdrew from Rwanda in December 1993, but a few dozen military advisors remained in the country. Not only did the extremist Rwandan government formed on April 8, 1994 receive French recognition and France's blessing, but the French ambassador also played a role in its establishment. Officially, France then ceased arming Rwandan government forces. In actuality, however, French weapons continued to find their way into the hands of the Rwandan military by way of Zaire. It took another month, until May 5, for the French government to officially decide to cease issuing weapon export permits for Rwanda, and doubts exist as to whether this decision was ever implemented.

On April 9, 1994, France flew troops into Rwanda to evacuate (white) foreign nationals. Although Tutsi who were married to Europeans were refused permission to board the planes, the evacuees did include a number of leaders of the old regime. Tutsi employees of the French embassy were abandoned and left to fend for themselves, and were subsequently murdered, as might have been expected. On April 12, 1994, the French ambassador closed the embassy in Rwanda and returned to Paris. Two days later, the last French soldiers left the building.

On April 22, 1994, a number of the leaders of the genocide visited France, including Rwandan Foreign Minister Jérôme Bicamumpaka, CDR leader Jean-Bosco Barayagwiza, and Protais Zigiranyirazo, the leader of the "death squads." President Mitterand and Foreign Minister Alain Juppé received them with honors, despite the genocide that was underway. It was on this occasion that General Jean-Pierre Huchon, the French military official responsible for aid to Rwanda, advised the visiting Rwandan officials to improve their "image."

France also provided support for the Rwandan government at the UN, where its representatives, like the representative of Rwanda's genocidal government, repeatedly argued that what was taking place in Rwanda was not genocide, but war. The blame therefore lay primarily with the RPF, they argued, and the government was not involved in the killings.

Furthermore, after the genocide, France helped some of the most prominent figures involved in the killings leave Rwanda. They included former prime minister Dismas Nsengiyaremye, a member of MDR-Hutu Power, and of the new government established on April 6, 1994; Defence Minister Augustin Bizimana; Professor Ferdinand Nahimana, minister of higher education, director of the RTLMC radio station, and a presidential advisor; and a number of other government ministers. Former First Lady Agathe Habyarimana and her brother Séraphin Rwabukumba, a prominent figure in the *Clan*, even received political asylum in France (Madame Habyarimana also received $40,000). In contrast, France refused to grant asylum to the five children of the moderate Hutu prime minister, who were subsequently murdered, along with their mother.

In June 1994, France initiated the establishment of a "safe zone" in Rwanda, and to this end dispatched 2,555 soldiers to southwest and northwest Rwanda. In order to give the French expeditionary force an appearance of international legitimacy, it was joined by a few dozen soldiers from Egypt, Senegal, Mauritania, Chad, and Guinea-Bissau. This measure, known as *Opération Turquoise*, was authorized by the UN Security Council on June 22, 1994. Its stated purpose was to create a "safe humanitarian zone" (*zone humanitaire sûre*) to protect the civilian population and to stop the massacres (the French spoke not of "genocide" but rather of "ethnic clashes").

In reality, the operation had other aims as well, including changing the unfavorable international reaction to France's policy and, apparently, saving the racist interim government in Rwanda and parts of the army, thus preventing the victory of the RPF, and making it possible to revert to the Arusha Accords and a shared government. During their presence in Rwanda, French forces saved approximately 15,000 Tutsi in the "safe zone." However, they also provided protection

Map 10: "The Safe Humanitarian Zone"

for the genocidal government, the RTLMC (which continued to broadcast from within the "safe zone" itself), the Rwandan army, and the leaders involved in the massacre.

In the French administration, the operation was the focus of a struggle between "hawks"—led by President Mitterand and his military advisor Christian Quesnot, who called for a realpolitik approach—and "doves"—led by Prime Minister Édouard Balladur, who was in favor of a limited humanitarian operation.

French policy remained hostile to the RPF even after Opération Turquoise, and provided no assistance to the new RPF government, which was established on July 18, 1994, after the defeat of the genocidal government. Its representatives were not invited to the French-African summit held in Biarritz on November 8–9, 1994. Moreover, France continued to pressure the new government to form a broad coalition with the MRNDD, the ruling party of the old regime.

Factors Influencing French Policy in Rwanda

Although Rwanda itself was never a French colony, France viewed it as part of the French sphere of influence in Africa—its "private hunting ground" (*chasse gardée*) or "grazing ground" (*pré carré*). It regarded Rwanda as a "solid base" (*base solide*) and important center for French political and economic influence in the region (Ndorimana 2001, 151). In the 1970s, President Valéry Giscard d'Estaing added the former Belgian territories of Congo, Rwanda, and Burundi, whose official language was French, to the Organisation Internationale de la Francophonie (OIF).

Therefore, members of the RPF, who were trained in Anglo-Saxon Uganda and spoke English, were said to pose a threat to the "Frenchness" of Rwanda. From this perspective, Mitterand regarded the RPF's war as partly a struggle against the Francophone zone in Africa. The fact that the Arusha Accords were concluded in Anglophone Tanzania is also relevant. Mitterand and his associates viewed the accords as an "Anglo-Saxon" conspiracy by Uganda, Tanzania, and the RPF, supported by the United States and Britain, and based on the intention of undermining French hegemony in the region. The French suspected that the US aimed to establish an American hegemony in the region because Zaire was a treasure of mineral resources (Ndorimana 2001, 151). In December 1994, French minister of cooperation Bernard Debré referred to the new Rwandan government as the "Anglo-Saxon Tutsi government from Uganda" (Ndorimana 2001, 340)."

France's Rwanda policy can be understood as a manifestation of its policy in Africa since 1960—a policy calling for "friendship" and support for all ruling dictators with whom it remained possible to conduct routine military, political, and economic business. It is no coincidence that while the genocide was still underway, Bruno Delay, Mitterand's advisor on African Affairs, uttered the words quoted at the beginning of this chapter: "You cannot deal with Africa [...] without getting your hands dirty."

One should also remember that the French ambassador in Kigali was known to be a confidant of Habyarimana, and that Habyarimana and Mitterand enjoyed close relations with one another, as did their sons Jean-Christophe Mitterand (who served as an advisor to his father on African affairs) and Jean-Pierre Habyarimana.

French policy toward Rwanda was bipartisan. It involved both President Mitterand and his confidants on the left, and government ministers on the right (Foreign Minister Alain Juppé, Cooperation Minister Bernard Debré, and others). In the case of France, close personal relationships and realpolitik appear to have outweighed all humanitarian and moral concerns.

In your opinion, which had a greater influence on France's attitude toward Rwanda—realpolitik calculations, moral and humanitarian concerns, or personal relationships?

Document: Flyer circulated in Butare prefecture at the time of Operation Turquoise.

"Tous les hommes regrettent la vie
lorsqu'elle leur échappe."

Les vrais amis sont rares, l'adversité les fait
connaître.

VIVE FRANÇOIS MITTERAND

VIVE LA COOPERATION FRANCO - RWANDAISE

VIVE LES MILITAIRES FRANÇAIS AU RWANDA

Illustration 8: A pamphlet distributed in Butare prefecture during Opération Turquoise

"All men value life more when their time is running out."
True friends are rare. We recognize them in times of trouble.
Long live François Mitterand
Long live Franco-Rwandan cooperation.
Long live the French soldiers in Rwanda.

BELGIAN POLICY ON THE GENOCIDE

Belgian authorities knew of the extent of the killing.
(Willy Claes[5] in Des Forges 1999, 620)

If Belgium had been courageous enough to leave our men there, we would have been able to save people.
(Lieutenant Luc Lemaire[6] in Des Forges 1999, 620)

Whereas France had Francophone interests in Rwanda, the interests of Belgium, which had ruled the country from 1918 to 1962, were those of a former colonial power (which could be defined as neocolonial in nature), and included investments, control of major market branches, the presence of commercial companies, the local concentration of businessmen, the provision of arms and military training, the work of lecturers and teachers in the local education system, missionary activities in the various churches operating in the country, and personal relationships between elites.

In April 1994, the 400 Belgian troops in Rwanda made up the largest contingent of the United Nations Assistance Mission to Rwanda (UNAMIR). Ten soldiers were killed on April 6, 1994 while unsuccessfully attempting to guard the Rwandan prime minister as she fled her home to the UN base (three soldiers were killed immediately, and seven were taken prisoner, tortured, and subsequently murdered). This resulted in Belgium's immediate decision to evacuate all its citizens from Rwanda, close its embassy there (which had managed to save only a few dozen priests and politicians), and withdraw its forces from UNAMIR. In order to maintain its dignity before the Belgian people and the world, the Belgian government worked for the withdrawal of the entire UNAMIR force (unless, it maintained, the force was to be significantly strengthened and given orders to intervene—a demand that would clearly be rejected by France, Britain, and the United States). Belgium no longer had any interest in a military presence in

---

[5] Belgian foreign minister during the genocide.

[6] A commander of the Belgian military force in Rwanda, in a testimony before the International Criminal Tribunal for Rwanda

the country. Even the Belgian branch of *Médecins sans frontières* left Rwanda at the beginning of the genocide. Between April 9 and 14, 1994, the Belgian army (with a force of approximately 850 soldiers) mounted an operation to evacuate (white) foreign citizens from Rwanda, while refusing to evacuate Tutsi who were fleeing for their lives, including those who had ties with Belgium, and even those who had worked for Belgian institutions.

The Belgian evacuation had an indirect impact on American policy toward Rwanda. One American diplomat asked how the US could get involved if the situation was so terrible that the Belgians were leaving.

When the Belgian government withdrew its forces from Rwanda, it was not under pressure from public opinion. Indeed, in a survey carried out in Belgium after the death of the ten Belgian soldiers, 48% of the respondents indicated support for maintaining the Belgian force in Rwanda and even reinforcing it, while 40% objected to a withdrawal, even in the event of additional Belgian casualties in the future. In another survey conducted in the Flemish region, 55% of respondents expressed their support for using the peacekeeping force to defend the Tutsi (although this survey also revealed that 80% opposed reinforcing the Belgian force).

Moreover, the Belgian parliamentary commission of inquiry heard the testimony of evacuated soldiers who had wanted to remain in Rwanda in order to put an end to the massacre, but had not been authorized to do so. Colonel Luc Marchal, head of the Kigali Command of UNAMIR forces during the genocide, would later write:

> Under no circumstances could we leave the country. This was the point of view that I expressed to my superiors until the moment when the political decision was made to leave UNAMIR. Our political leaders should have known that in leaving UNAMIR, we would condemn thousands of men, women and children to certain death. (Des Forges 1999, 620)

It should be noted that the evacuated Belgian force was the best-trained and best-equipped UN force in the country at the time. It was also very knowledgeable about the different areas of Rwanda and the events taking place there. After all, as a former colonial power in Rwanda, Belgium had detailed information on the country that Bangladesh (which contributed troops to UNAMIR) or even France did not have. Indeed, the withdrawal of Belgian forces proved a serious blow to the overall UN force in the country.

In contrast to its attitude towards the French, the defunct Rwandan old regime detested the Belgians. Unlike the French, the Belgians enjoyed good relations with the government that had been established by the RPF. Between July 1994 and August 1995, the new government was led by moderate MDR leader Faustin Twagiramungu, former director of the Brussels office of the RPF and leader of the bloc of four opposition parties.

US POLICY ON THE GENOCIDE

Zero degree of involvement and zero degree of risk and zero degree of pain and confusion.

> (David Obey[7] in Burkhalter 1994/1995, 44–45)

On April 16, a US diplomat told the Belgian ambassador that it was 'unacceptable' that concern for a 'humanitarian drama' be used to justify keeping the peacekeeping force in Rwanda. If such arguments were to be used, it might make other peacekeeping operations 'unworkable.'

> (Des Forges 1999, 630)

Come on, Boutros, relax [...] don't put us in a difficult position [...] The mood is not for intervention, you will obtain nothing [...] We will not move.

> (Madeleine Albright[8] in Martin 2002, 20)

We cannot solve every such outburst of civil strife or militant nationalism simply by sending in our forces [...] Whether we get involved in any of the world's ethnic conflicts in the end must depend on the cumulative weight of the American interests at stake.

> (President Bill Clinton at the Naval Academy in Annapolis, Maryland, May 25, 1994.)

---

[7] American Congressman on the American policy in Rwanda.

[8] US ambassador to the UN.

As the above quotes demonstrate, the United States did not intervene in the events unfolding in Rwanda. President Clinton, who during his 1992 election campaign had praised his country's commitment to "humanitarian intervention" in disaster-stricken areas around the world, was actually the primary opponent to US intervention in the country. The United States did not even send marines to Rwanda to evacuate its own citizens; the Europeans did that for them. The American ambassador closed the doors of the American embassy on April 10, 1994, without attempting to help his Tutsi employees or acquaintances.

For a period of two months, the United States refused to acknowledge that the events unfolding in Rwanda constituted "genocide." Indeed, the State Department even barred its officials from using the very term, in order not to force the administration to take action in accordance with the UN Convention on the Prevention and Punishment of the Crime of Genocide. For this very reason, they spoke of "war," "civil war," "civil strife," "anarchy," and "chaos," but only on rare occasions of "acts of genocide." On May 26, 1994, the State Department spokesperson announced that the question of whether or not the events taking place in Rwanda did in fact constitute genocide was under consideration. But only after June 10, 1994, when the *New York Times* focused public attention on the State Department's instructions to American diplomats around the world, did Secretary of State Warren Christopher issue a statement that "genocide" was in fact the appropriate term for what had taken place in Rwanda.

At a meeting of the UN Security Council on April 21, 1994, the United States supported full evacuation of UNAMIR, in which the US had refused to participate (it was ultimately decided to reduce the force to 250 soldiers), while opposing the expansion of the force's operational authority. On May 17, 1994, when it was decided to dispatch a new UN force to Rwanda (UNAMIR II), the United States again refused to take part in the initiative. In order to do the minimum expected of them, American officials agreed to send fifty Armored Personnel Carriers (APCs), which took seven weeks to arrive in the region, and which were ultimately delivered to Uganda instead of Rwanda (Power 2001, 105). Finally, on May 26, 1994, the United States did impose an arms embargo on both sides—the genocidal government and the RPF.

The APC Affair

On May 19, 1994, at the height of the genocide, the UN requested fifty APCs for UNAMIR II. On May 31, the US announced its agreement in principle. For the next three weeks, until May 31, officials in the Pentagon and the UN bickered over financial questions (such as whether the APCs should be sold or leased to the UN and who would pay for transport) and technical issues (such as whether the vehicles would be tracked or wheeled). According to the policies of the Pentagon, the vehicles could not be prepared until a contract was signed. June 19, 1994 marked the beginning of the transport of the APCs, which lacked heavy machine guns and radios. Between June 23 and June 30, the vehicles finally arrived (without this crucial equipment), not in Rwanda, however, but in Uganda.

American officials thus chose not to send military aid to a region where full-blown genocide was taking place. But, that is not all. They even refused to disrupt the deadly radio broadcasts of the RTLMC, despite the fact that the Pentagon possessed the equipment to do so and that the job would have required no military intervention.

In response to a request by Human Rights Watch that the US disrupt the incendiary broadcasts, the State Department appointed a committee of legal experts, which concluded that such action could not be taken because it violated international agreements and the principle of freedom of expression (Des Forges 1999, 641; Prunier 1995, 99). The testimony of a Pentagon official on this issue speaks for itself; for example, on May 5, 1994, Frank Wisner, Undersecretary for Defence Policy, commented in a memo to Deputy National Security Advisor Sandy Berger:

> We have looked at options to stop the broadcasts within the Pentagon, discussed them interagency and concluded jamming is an ineffective and expensive mechanism that will not accomplish the objective the NSC Advisor seeks.

International legal conventions complicate airborne or ground based jamming and the mountainous terrain reduces the effectiveness of either option. Commando Solo, an Air National Guard asset, is the only suitable DOD jamming platform. It costs approximately $8500 per flight hour and requires a semi-secure area of operations due to its vulnerability and limited self-protection.

I believe it would be wiser to use air to assist in Rwanda in the (food) relief effort. (Burkhalter, 1994/1995, 44–54)

The lack of acknowledgment of the impact of use of radio broadcasting in disseminating ideas that were fomenting genocide is evident, too, in response to a request made by Prudence Bushnell, Deputy Assistant Secretary of State for African Affairs, that radio broadcasts should be jammed, a senior Pentagon official declared: "Radios don't kill people. People kill people" (Burkhalter, 1994/1995, 44–54).

The United States, which did nothing to prevent the genocide, maintained relations with the provisional government that carried out the genocide until July 15, 1994, when the RPF ousted the genocidal government and gained full control of Rwanda. Only then, three months after the onset of the genocide, was the Rwandan embassy in Washington closed and the embassy staff expelled, and only then did the American delegation to the UN express its support for removing Rwanda's representative to the UN Security Council.

Despite America's unequivocally non-interventionist policy, a number of different voices on the events taking place in Rwanda could be heard within the administration and Congress. Some, as we have seen, strongly supported a policy of non-intervention (based on the assertion that intervention advanced no "vital national interests"). They included President Clinton, the secretary of state, and the deputy secretary of state; the secretary of defence; the national security advisor; and Senate Republican opposition leader Bob Dole. The United States had no Tutsi community, so that there was no lobby for intervention. African American congress members also failed to take action on behalf of the Tutsi. At the time, they were engaged in the crisis in Haiti, which was closer to home.[9] In this context, American public opinion, too, did not put pressure on the government to intervene in Rwanda.

At the same time, however, a number of congress members and administration officials were calling for American involvement in Rwanda to prevent genocide—calls which ultimately proved unsuccessful. They included the head of the State Department's Bureau of African Affairs, the National Security Council director for Africa, and the chairpersons of the Senate and House committees on African affairs. On May 13, 1994, Senators Paul Simon (D, Illinois) and James Jeffords (R, Vermont), both members of the US Senate Foreign Relations Committee, wrote to President Clinton requesting that the US urgently demand that the UN send troops to Rwanda to stop the carnage. Clinton replied, after twenty-seven days (!), on June 9, that he agrees. By then, however, the genocide was nearly complete (Martin 2002, 20).

What motivated this US policy of non-intervention? With the end of the Cold War, the United States clearly had no vital national interest in Rwanda—not on a military strategic level, not on a global political level (as it did during the Cold War), and not on an economic level. Nor was the administration interested in "another Somalia."[10] Indeed, the April 6, 1994 murder of ten Belgian soldiers in Rwanda served as a sign to the Americans that if they intervened, they would run the risk of entanglement, similar to what they had encountered in Somalia. Fear of another long drawn-out campaign after the wars in Vietnam[11]

---

[9]   The democratic regime of Father Jean-Bertrand Aristide of the black nation of Haiti, which is located close to the United States, was overthrown by a military coup in September 1991. American forces arrived in Haiti in 1994 to restore democracy. American interest in Haiti stemmed from its geographical proximity, its Afro-American population, the large Haitian population in the US, and the tens of thousands of Haitian refugees who were trying to reach the United States.

[10]   In Somalia in 1993, eighteen Marines were killed and dragged through the streets of Mogadishu in the aftermath of an American military operation aimed at halting internal fighting and famine in the country.

[11]   Between 1964 and 1973, the United States was deeply embroiled in a bloody war in Vietnam, aimed at preventing the communist conquest of the southern part of the country and the unification of the north and the south. The high casualty rate (56,000 Americans) and the stinging military defeat caused a profound national trauma and reinforced American isolationist tendencies and objection to all military intervention in foreign lands.

and Iraq-Kuwait,[12] while in the midst of intervention crises in Bosnia and Haiti, also appear to have played an important role in shaping this policy. It is important to emphasize once more that, despite his statements during the election campaign, President Clinton proved unwilling to send troops to Rwanda on the basis of humanitarian considerations only. This decision was undoubtedly also influenced by economic factors, as such intervention would have been expensive and apparently unpopular in Congress at the time. Nor were there any clear domestic political considerations (such as pressure from Congress, the African American lobby, or public opinion) to outweigh a realpolitik that discouraged intercession solely for the sake of saving a forgotten people in a distant land in the heart of Black Africa. This was, without a doubt, a moral failure, as President Clinton acknowledged four years later.

The Clinton Apology
(Rwanda, March 1998)

We come here today partly in recognition of the fact that we in the United States and the world community did not do as much as we could have and should have done to try to limit what occurred in Rwanda (Power 2001, 85).

It is important to remember that only after the Rwandan genocide had become an established fact did the United States send thousands of soldiers to the region (Zaire and Rwanda) to help the masses of refugees by supplying food, water, and medical supplies.

---

[12]   In August 1990, Iraq, under the leadership of Saddam Hussein, invaded Kuwait, based on the claim that the country was a "historic" part of Iraq. Iraq's occupation of Kuwait raised concerns regarding future Iraqi invasions of other countries in the region. In face of the threat of Iraqi seizure of oil wealth throughout the Middle East and the practical threat posed to regional stability, the United States dispatched 500,000 troops to the region. In the subsequent war that was fought in January-February 1991, the United States succeeded in ejecting the Iraqi army from Kuwait, sustaining only minimal losses in the process.

Compare and analyze French, Belgian, and American policies during the genocide in Rwanda.

UN POLICY ON THE GENOCIDE

UNAMIR will take the necessary action to prevent any crime against humanity.

(Roméo Dallaire[13] in Des Forges 1999, 133)

Give me the means and I can do more.

(Roméo Dallaire[14] in Power 2001, 598)

Nobody in New York was interested in that.

(Maurice Baril[15] in Power 2001, 598)

As noted, the Arusha Accords of August 1993 specified the establishment of a UN force to maintain peace and security in Rwanda. Both sides requested that 8,000 troops be sent to the country; the Canadian commander of the UN force, General Roméo Dallaire, recommended the dispatch of 4,500 soldiers; the United States proposed making do with 500 troops; and the UN Security Council eventually authorized 2,548. In practice, the UNAMIR force that arrived in Rwanda in December 1993 consisted of only 1,260 soldiers. The force—made up of soldiers from Belgium, Ghana, and Bangladesh (the latter, however, were undisciplined and devoid of any military skills)—was not properly equipped: it lacked armed personnel carriers and ambulances and suffered from a constant shortage of ammunition, food, and medical supplies. The Security Council also diluted UNAMIR's mandate as opposed to what had been decided on in the Arusha Accords, with disastrous consequences.[16]

---

[13] Canadian commander of the UN peacekeeping force in Rwanda.

[14] General Dallaire's plea to his superiors at UN headquarters in New York.

[15] General Baril's response to General Dallaire.

[16] For primary sources on the Arusha Accords and the UN Resolution, see respectively http://www.incore.ulst.ac.uk/services/cds/agreements/pdf/rwan1.pdf, and http://www.un.org/Docs/scres/1993/scres93.htm

Arusha Accords (4 August 1993)	UN Security Council Resolution (5 October 1993)
"Guarantee the overall security of the country and especially verify the maintenance of law and order by the competent authorities and organs."	"To contribute to the security of the city of Kigali inter alia within a weapons-secure area established by the parties in and around the city; To monitor observance of the cease-fire agreement"
"Assist in the tracking of arms caches and neutralization of armed gangs throughout the country" and "Assist in the recovery of all weapons distributed to, or illegally acquired by civilians."	"To assist with mine clearance, primarily through training programmes."
"Assist in catering for the security of civilians."	"To investigate and report on incidents regarding the activities of the gendarmerie and police."

Table 8: The mandate of the UN Force in Rwanda (Burkhalter 1994, 17–27; Des Forges 1999, 132, 596)

How does the Security Council resolution differ from the Arusha Accords? Do they reflect different aims?

The UN establishment was well aware of the course events in Rwanda could potentially take. In August 1993, the UN special rapporteur for Rwanda warned that genocide was liable to take place in the country. In December 1993, General Dallaire received reliable reports from Rwandan officers regarding an evolving conspiracy to carry out genocide. On January 11, 1994, Dallaire informed the UN General Secretary about intelligence reports regarding preparations to murder the Tutsi population in the capital city of Kigali. His report included information about the registration of all Tutsi in preparation for a "final solution." Dallaire explained that his source (who went under the name "Jean-Pierre"), a former member of the president's security services, had told him that they were planning to kill the Tutsi at a rate of 3,000 people per hour. Jean-Pierre also informed Dallaire of a plan to murder a number of Belgian UN soldiers in order to bring about a rapid Belgian withdrawal from the region (a plan that was implemented on April 6, 1994) (Power 2001, 89). In his report, Dallaire requested an expansion of the mandate of the powerless UN force, including the authority to confiscate weapons.

All of Dallaire's requests were denied by Iqbal Riza, the deputy of Kofi Annan of Ghana, who was then serving as the director of the UN Department of Peacekeeping Operations.[17] Moreover, Dallaire's report and requests were not even relayed to the Security Council. UN Secretary General Boutros Boutros-Ghali of Egypt tended to give more credence to the reports of his political representative in Rwanda, Jacques-Roger Booh Booh of Cameroon, who was sympathetic to the Rwandan Hutu regime and referred to the anti-Tutsi mob attacks as "violent clashes." In light of their experiences between November 1993 and April 1994, the planners of the genocide appear to have concluded that the UN force was an impotent organization with no authority, and as such posed no threat to them, no matter what they did.

Indeed, when put to the test, the UN force in Rwanda failed to protect the Tutsi, who were murdered before their very eyes. Although it assigned guards to protect moderate Hutu leaders, they typically abandoned them when the militias actually arrived, planning to kill them. General Dallaire urgently requested that his force be increased in order to enable him to confiscate weapons, stop the killing, and jam the broadcasts of the RTLMC. All his requests, however, were denied by the UN Department of Peacekeeping Operations, which issued him with explicit instructions to refrain from using force, from endangering his soldiers, from confiscating weapons, from acting against the radio stations, and ordered him to maintain absolute neutrality. At the time, Kofi Annan maintained that expanding the force would be too expensive and that such measures did not have the

---

[17] Kofi Annan was born in Ghana in 1938 and studied economics, international relations, and management in his home country and in the United States. When he joined the UN administration in 1962, most of his responsibilities were in the realm of finances and economics. In 1990, he was asked by the UN secretary general to mediate on humanitarian issues that surfaced during the Gulf War. In light of his success in this capacity, he was appointed Under-Secretary-General for Peacekeeping Operations. In late 1996, Anan was confirmed as the replacement of the outgoing UN secretary general, a position he held until the end of 2006. He was awarded the Nobel Peace Prize in 2001.

support of the Americans (which was true). Instead, the Department of Peacekeeping Operations suggested to an infuriated Dallaire that he should help UN personnel evacuate the country along with the European rescue force.[18] Even when the killings in Rwanda were at their height, neither the organs of the UN nor the members of the Security Council considered taking steps to expel the Rwandan representative from the Council.

During the deliberations on Rwanda, conducted by the Security Council on April 21, April 30, and May 17, 1994, three groups of countries, dissimilar with regard to their positions on the issue, emerged, as seen in Table 9 on the following page.

Policy was ultimately determined by the position reflected in the third column of the table: i.e. a policy of neutrality and non-intervention. The other two positions neutralized one another. As we have seen, the UN administration itself (Secretary General Boutros Boutros-Ghali; Kofi Annan, director of the UN Department of Peacekeeping Operations; and Jacques-Roger Booh Booh, his representative in Rwanda) also tended to support "neutrality."

On April 21, 1994, the Security Council decided to reduce UNAMIR from 1,260 to 250 soldiers; the secretary general supported not only the complete evacuation of the force, but also the exertion of pressure on General Dallaire himself to call for its evacuation (Dallaire refused to do so for moral reasons). On April 30, 1994, the president of the Security Council called for an arms embargo on both sides; it was imposed in Resolution 918 on May 17.

---

18   Dallaire's experience in Rwanda caused him intense psychological trauma that was to remain with him for years to come. His conscience tormented him because he had not disregarded the orders of his superiors, a failure for which he was later criticized by French and Belgian military and political officials (who themselves took no action during the genocide). He was discharged from the Canadian army in April 2000 for medical reasons, and subsequently became a Canadian senator for the province of Québec.

Position	Support of Rwanda	Take action to stop the genocide	Maintain neutrality
Permanent Members			
China			X
Russia			X
United States			X
United Kingdom			X
France	X		
Non-Permanent Members			
Djibouti	X		
Oman	X		
Rwanda	X		
Argentina		X	
Czech Republic		X	
New Zealand		X	
Spain		X	
Brazil			X
Nigeria			X
Pakistan			X

Table 9: Positions of UN Security Council members on the Genocide in Rwanda

As noted, it was not until May 17 that the Security Council resolved to send a reconstituted, 5,500 member force to Rwanda (UNAMIR II). At that point, no non-African countries were willing to contribute soldiers to the UN force, and the few African countries that agreed to do so first negotiated for significant financial compensation. As a result of this sluggish process, the UN force hardly managed to save any Tutsi. As we have seen, a Rwandan representative continued to sit on the Security Council during the entire period, and both the Rwandan foreign minister and the leader of the CDR (who were among the architects and leaders of the genocide) arrived in New York for the Security Council deliberations of May 16–17. Apparently, it never occurred to anyone, neither in the UN nor in the US, to prevent them from making the trip or to arrest them at the airport. For months, the UN refrained from classifying the massacres in Rwanda as "genocide," as such classification would have drawn public attention to the institution's failure to take action.

The term was first applied to the Rwandan context in late June 1994, as reflected in the following chronology:

April 8, 1994	UN representative in Rwanda, Jacques-Roger Booh Booh, reports "fighting" in Kigali and "calm, although tense" conditions throughout the rest of the country.
April 20, 1994	In a special report to the Security Council, UN Secretary General Boutros Boutros-Ghali speaks of the "the critical situation in Rwanda," saying that "the killings were started by unruly members of the Presidential Guard" and noting that "authority collapsed."
April 21, 1994	In Resolution 912, the Security Council stated that it was "appalled at the large-scale violence in Rwanda, which has resulted in the death of thousands of innocent civilians" (without specifying who was doing the killing).
April 29, 1994	In a letter to the President of the Security Council, the UN secretary general acknowledges that the killing of innocent civilians is distinct from war, and that the massacres had been carried out by "armed groups of civilians" and by "uncontrolled military" (in fact, they were extremely well controlled). In this way, he continued to obscure the fact that the killing was government directed.
April 30, 1994	In a statement issued by the President of the Security Council, he cites the Convention on the Prevention and Punishment of the Crime of Genocide, "The Security Council condemns all these breaches of international humanitarian law in Rwanda [...] In this context, the Security Council recalls that the killing of members of an ethnic group with the intention of destroying such a group in whole or in part constitutes a crime punishable under international law." He refrains, however, from classifying the events in Rwanda as genocide.
May 17, 1994	In Resolution 918, the Security Council reiterates the statement by the President of the Council of April 30, 1994.

May 25, 1994	The UN Commission on Human Rights indicates that "genocidal acts may have occurred" in Rwanda (and asks that a special rapporteur be appointed to investigate and report back on the matter).
June 28, 1994	In his report to the Commission, Special Rapporteur René Degni-Segni confirms that acts of genocide had in fact taken place, "In the Special Rapporteur's view, the term 'genocide' should henceforth be used as regards the Tutsi."
July 26, 1994	The UN Secretary General convenes a Commission of Experts (consisting of representatives of Togo, Guinea, and Mali) to confirm reports of "grave violations of international humanitarian law committed in the territory of Rwanda, including the evidence of possible acts of genocide."
October 1994	The Commission concludes that "Acts of genocide against the Tutsi group were perpetrated by Hutu elements in a concerted, planned, systematic and methodical way." It recommends that the "individuals responsible" be "brought to justice before an independent and impartial international criminal tribunal."
November 8, 1994	In Resolution 955, the Security Council decides to establish a special "international tribunal for the sole purpose of prosecuting persons responsible for genocide . . . ."

Table 10: Genocide in Rwanda: Evolution of a Term (Des Forges 1999, 626–639; Magnarella 2000; Ingvar Carlsson, Han Sun-Joo, and Kupolati 1999)

Summarize the various explanations for the behavior of the UN.

THE POLICY OF THE AFRICAN COUNTRIES ON THE GENOCIDE

In the case of Rwanda, neither the countries of Africa, nor the regional *Communauté économique des pays des Grands Lacs*, nor the Organization of African Unity (OAU) behaved in a manner the African continent could possibly have been proud of.[19] Like many of the other countries discussed above, the OAU (whose president at the time was Egyptian president Husni Mubarak) also refused to speak in terms of "genocide." In fact, the organization even permitted Théodore Sindikubwabo, the president of the genocidal regime, to represent Rwanda at the African summit convention in Tunis in mid-June 1994. Participants at the conference condemned instances of "crimes against humanity," without specifying who committed them and without referring explicitly to genocide. The Africa Group in the United Nations, consisting of all African member countries, also failed to work in a determined manner to stop the genocide (although it did call for a "cease-fire" on April 11, 1994 and opposed the reduction of UNAMIR on April 21, 1994).

In the Security Council, Nigeria chose neither to attack the Rwandan government nor to charge it with genocide, while Djibouti, for its part, maintained its support of Rwanda throughout the crisis. Some African countries—Zaire (today the Democratic Republic of Congo), Kenya, and Seychelles in particular—even supplied Rwanda with weapons after April 6, 1994. Kenya and Zaire also refused to allow Tutsi to escape across the border into their territory, and Kenya even handed over refugees who had managed to cross the border, straight into the hands of the murderers. In this context, it is

---

[19] The Organization of African Unity (OAU) was established in 1963 as an organization of independent states on the African continent. It included all the independent countries of Arab North Africa and sub-Saharan Africa. With the eventual inclusion of post-Apartheid South Africa, the OAU encompassed fifty-one sovereign countries. Since its inception, the OAU has been engaged in assisting African liberation movements; mediating between war-torn African countries; promoting economic development, education, and health care throughout Africa; coordinating among African countries in aviation, communications, and cooperation with the UN and other international organizations. The OAU's administrative center was located in the Ethiopian capital of Addis Ababa. In 2002, the OAU was replaced by the African Union, a new organization that attempted to emulate the European Union.

of the utmost importance to emphasize the inactivity of the African triumvirate in the upper echelons of the UN—Boutros Boutros-Ghali of Egypt, Kofi Annan of Ghana, and Jacques-Roger Booh Booh of Cameroon, who did nothing to prevent the genocide.

The safe havens to which senior Rwandan officials eventually fled (see Table 11) also reflects the positions of these African countries on the genocide. Kenya and Cameroon, for example, were prominent countries that accepted murderers.

Name	Position	Destination
Agathe Habyarimana	wife of the President	Kenya (after an interim stop in France)
Augustin Bizimana	Minister of Defence (organized and armed the militias)	Kenya
Casimir Bizimungu	Minister of Health (organized murders in hospitals)	Kenya
Félicien Kabuga	bankroller and Director of the RTLMC	Kenya
André Ntagerura	Minister of Transportation (responsible for the killings in the Karengera region)	Kenya
Justin Mugenzi	Minister of Commerce	Cameroon
Joseph Nzirorera	MRNDD secretary general	Cameroon
Colonel Théoneste Bagosora	The "strong man" of the genocide regime	Cameroon

Table 11: Destinations of senior Rwandan government officials

---

Why do you think the countries of Africa failed to come to the aid of the people who were being slaughtered?

COULD THE WORLD
HAVE PREVENTED THE GENOCIDE?

UNAMIR in combination with the evacuation force
"could easily have stopped the massacres and showed the
people at the barriers that it was dangerous to be there.
They would have gone home."

(Roméo Dallaire[20] in Des Forges 1999, 607)

For the world to be able to prevent genocide, it first has to know about it. No one denies that in the Rwandan case everyone knew about the "final solution"—the incitement, the organization, and the distribution of weapons. When the genocide began, the developments were known to the foreign ambassadors in Rwanda, to aid agency employees, UNAMIR soldiers and commanders, and to leaders of the administrations in Paris, Brussels, Washington, and the UN.

The commission of inquiry on Rwanda, set up by the OAU in 1998 and headed by former Botswana president Sir Ketumile Masire, characterized the genocide in Rwanda as a "preventable genocide," as did Howard Adelman, who described the Rwandan genocide as "the most easily preventable genocide one can imagine" (Adelman 2000, 431–444). It should not have been difficult to prevent, particularly in view of the binding convention aimed at preventing genocides, the presence of a UN force in the country, the murderers' lack of heavy weaponry, and the fact that the campaign was led by a mere few thousand people.

As we have seen, UNAMIR Commander General Dallaire never had any doubt that a few thousand, well-trained troops could have stopped the genocide. In his opinion, the Belgian and Ghanaian troups (which numbered 440 and 1,000 soldiers respectively)—reinforced by the Franco-Belgian evacuation force (900 soldiers),

---

[20] UNAMIR Commander.

the US marines stationed in the Burundian capital of Bujumbura (300 marines), and an additional Belgian force then stationed in Nairobi—could easily have overcome the 7,000 Rwandan soldiers in Kigali, thus stopping the genocide and preventing its spread to other parts of the country. He also maintained that the Rwandans would not even have fought an international force containing a French contingent. Among other things, Dallaire argued that UNAMIR alone, without any additional help, could have accomplished a great deal had it been quickly provided with the proper equipment and given the green light to take offensive action. A number of military experts shared Dallaire's view. For example, President Mitterand's military advisor, General Christian Quesnot, who was extremely knowledgeable about the Rwandan army, estimated that the massacre could have been halted by 2,500 determined and well-trained men (Des Forges 1999, 607). American officers and intelligence officials also shared this assessment. In a report prepared for the Carnegie Commission, Colonel Scott Feil of the US army wrote the following:

> A modern force of 5,000 troops [...] sent to Rwanda sometime between April 7 and April 21, 1994, could have significantly altered the outcome of the conflict [...] Forces appropriately trained, equipped and commanded, and introduced in a timely manner, could have stemmed the violence in and around the capital, prevented its spread to the countryside, and created conditions conducive to the cessation of the civil war between the Rwandan Patriotic Front (RPF) and the Rwandan Government Forces (RGF). (African Union 2000)

Without a doubt, the country's size and good network of roads would have made possible a rescue operation that could have reached every focal point of the killings quickly. In addition, Western intelligence sources had received reports that some Rwandan officers would have joined the anti-genocidal effort of an international force—had one been initiated.

Scholars are not in complete agreement on this point, however. For example, Kuperman argues that there was no chance that Rwandan officers would have supported an international force (2000, 94). This was due, he claims, to the fact that the rapid pace of the murders made it nearly impossible to stop them in practice, and that the Americans did not receive reports on the genocide until April 20, 1994. Kuperman fails to explain why the Americans failed to take action once they did receive the reports. In his view, only an extremely large force would have been capable of stopping the massacre.

In any event, the Rwandan government was dependent on foreign aid to feed its population, pay its employees, and arm its military. It therefore stands to reason that a world determined to take action could have deterred Rwanda from implementing the "final solution." In fact, the Rwandan government knew very well that it was facing an indifferent world—motivated largely by narrow interests—that would do nothing to prevent it from carrying out its plans.

Illustration 9: "What happened to the Tutsi in 1994." (Drawn by a boy who survived the genocide.)

Rwanda

The eyes burn,
the nose itches,
the belly craves,
and
the bones in the wrists, ankles, and legs
throb—
but the joys of the body are not unknown
as the mind grows,
and perhaps
even a little wisdom is honed.

I wake breathless in the morning,
deep from the warmth of sleep,
I hear the birds chirping in the dark,
think about God,
wonder what it is all about,
name my ten gratitudes,
try not to be cynical
or shrewd,

try to remember the surge of spring in the veins,
the passions, the love.

All calm now,
tempered
with disbelieving
almost everything taught to me
by man.

What a brain-wash it all is,
steeped in the illusions of "our way"
which is the way
that has led the world to such
a catastrophe as
Rwanda.

Saw a movie last night on the million dead,
created by our greed,
our culture,
our Christianity.

The solution?

Forget the UN, propagated by our
commerce.
Take all the Western Colonialists
(who thrive more today then ever)
add them to all the Western-educated

Rwandans,
and put them out of their misery.

Perhaps then the 10,000 years of peace
will descend on Africa again.

When our civilization has failed completely
as a humanitarian enterprise,
why do we still think we can solve
the problems we have
created?

We don't.
We,
the generals and the suited elite,
enjoy the problems
as "the great game"
like the British were playing
all around the world
in the old days,
destroying one culture after another.

Enter.
Divide.
Incite racial hatred—
and they'll kill each other.
While we stand by moaning our Christian hymns,
mouthing our hypocritical paeans of peace.

Whoever made enough money at war-games
in peacetime?

Greed is the creed.
Even though the birds still sing
in the pre-dawn light.

(Jan Haag, 1997)

4

THE RWANDAN GENOCIDE IN COMPARATIVE PERSPECTIVE

I do not see any difference between what is happening in Rwanda and what happened in Germany between 1940 and 1945.

(Faustin Twagiramungu[1] in Klinghoffer 1998, 115)

The genocide in Rwanda is the most horrifying human tragedy to occur since the Holocaust.

(Paul Kagame[2] in Klinghoffer 1998, 115)

In Germany, the Jews were taken out of their residences, moved to distant far away locations, and killed there, almost anonymously. In Rwanda, the government did not kill. It prepared the population, enraged it and enticed it. Your neighbors killed you [...] In Germany, if the population participated in the killing, it was not directly but indirectly. If the neighbor's son killed, it is because he joined the army.

(Patrick Mazimpaka[3] in Mamdani 2001, 6)

This chapter explores the similarities and differences between the genocide that took place in Rwanda and two other, infamous genocides: the Armenian and the Jewish genocide. These two genocides should help us better understand what happened in Rwanda. In fact, any serious academic study of the Rwandan genocide must also consider comparisons drawn by social scientists, politicians, and diplomats.

---

[1]   Prime Minister-designate of Rwanda.

[2]   Vice-president of Rwanda.

[3]   RPF Rwandan government minister.

- An important general distinction between different instances of genocide is offered by Palmer, who distinguishes between "state genocide," or genocide carried out by state authorities, and "societal genocide," or genocide perpetrated by society or parts of society, without governmental involvement. Other scholars maintain that behind the scenes all genocides are initiated, planned, and legitimized by a state (Uvin 206). Clearly, the three cases of genocide under discussion here (Jewish, Armenian, and Rwandan) were instances of state genocide, resulting not from a "spontaneous" outburst of mass violence but from deliberate policy. Still, in the Rwandan case—unlike in the other two cases—hundreds of thousands of rank and file citizens took part in the murders, along with an organized killing apparatus (army, gendarmerie, and militias). From this perspective, it was a case of a "people killing another people" (Chalk 1996, 14–17).

- In all three cases, the victims were members of minority groups that were relatively educated, successful, and affluent, or, in other words, groups against which it was relatively easy to incite the general population. Unlike in colonial genocides (such as the murder of the native peoples of the American continent, the Aborigines of Australia, and the Herero people of German South-West Africa),[4] the majority and the minority in the genocides discussed here were members of the same society, with common ties of culture and civilization. In the Jewish and Rwandan instances, there were even numerous cases of intermarriage between the two groups. Another similarity between them was the use of a racist ideology against the victims. Indeed, in both cases it was racist ideology that provided the underpinning of the campaign of extermination. On the basis of this ideology, both the Jews and the Tutsi were demonized and dehumanized as overassertive foreigners and parasites.

- All three genocides took place in wartime, so that war provided a convenient rationale for the killings. One can, nonetheless, distinguish between the types of "logic" that provided alleged justifications for the genocides. In the Jewish case, members

---

4   Modern-day Namibia.

of the Nazi leadership were convinced that they were battling "world Jewry," and that it was therefore necessary to kill all Jews, wherever they lived. The Armenian genocide was also justified by a war-related logic of sorts, as the Turkish murderers charged the Armenians with ties with the Russian enemy and claimed that, as an oppressed minority in Turkey, the Armenians were anxiously waiting for their liberation by Russian troops. The logic was similar in the case of Rwanda, as many Hutu undoubtedly regarded the Rwandan Patriotic Front (RPF) as a threat to the Hutu state. Hutu fear of the Tutsi greatly increased after the mutual Hutu-Tutsi massacres that took place in Burundi after the October 1993 assassination of Burundi's Hutu president, Melchior Ndadaye.

- In all three cases, the victims belonged to groups with a separate collective consciousness, and two of the three, the Armenians and the Jews (though not the Tutsi), practiced a different religion from that of the majority. The Armenians and the Jews of Eastern Europe (but not the Jews of Germany, nor the Tutsi of Rwanda) also spoke distinct languages. The people who carried out the genocide were aware of the different collective identity of their victims.

- All were cases of mass killings, not selective political terrorism (except for the murder of moderate Hutu in the Rwandan context).

- And, in all three, a distinction was made between the "settlers" or "foreigners" on the one hand and the "locals" on the other to justify the genocidal acts, although the nature of the link differed in each instance. In the Armenian case, the Turks, who had settled in Turkey hundreds of years earlier, murdered the "indigenous population," which had settled there before them. However, during the Jewish and Rwandan genocides, the tables turned, as the "locals" killed the "foreigners," whether their foreignness was real or imagined. The Jews were perceived as a foreign element with a corrupting influence on German society, and the Tutsi were regarded as Hamitic occupiers, who had in the past conquered the Hutu.

- The killings were always followed by the perpetrators' attempts to deny their actions. However, in contrast to the relatively marginal phenomenon of Holocaust denial in Germany, denial by the perpetrators in the Rwandan and Armenian cases (the Hutu and the Turks) was sweeping.

The genocide in Rwanda differed from the Jewish and the Armenian genocides, thus making it unique in a number of ways: the frenetic pace of the killings (the genocide was carried out in just 100 days); the primitive technology with which it was mostly carried out (machetes, clubs, stones, and fire); international awareness that the genocide was about to take place; its preventability; the presence of a UN force in the country; and worldwide, real-time media broadcasts about the genocide.

Genocide Characteristics	Victims		
	Jews	**Armenians**	**Tutsi**
State planning and organization	+	+	+
Instructions from above	+	+	+
Efficient and disciplined implementation apparatus	+	+	+
Formal exterminationist/eliminationist ideology	+	−	+
Wartime context	+	+	+
Industrial extermination	+	−	−
Extermination camps	+	−	−
Murder of women and children	+	+	+
Mobilization of local authorities to facilitate extermination	−	+	+
Widespread use of media to facilitate extermination	−	−	+
False propaganda	+	+	+
Victims belonged to a minority group living among a majority population	+	+	+
Image of victims as affluent, successful, and educated	+	+	+
Minority isolated from society prior to extermination	+	+	+
General population participated in the killings	−	−	+
World indifference to the genocide as it unfolded	+	+	+
A number of murderers were punished	+	−	+
Majority society's sweeping denial of the genocide	−	+	+

Table 12: Comparison of the Jewish Holocaust, the Armenian genocide, and the genocide in Rwanda

5

THE CAUSES OF
THE RWANDAN GENOCIDE

*My obedience makes me part of the power I worship . . . I
can make no error, since it decides for me.*

(Erich Fromm in Hintjens 1999, 272)

*In Rwandan culture, everyone obeys authority. People
revere power, and there isn't enough education. You take
a poor, ignorant population and give them arms, and say
"It's yours. Kill." They'll obey.*

(François-Xavier Nkurunziza[1] in Mamdani 2001, 200)

*In Kibirira they [the officials] told Hutu to kill their Tutsi
neighbors to fulfill their umuganda obligation for the
month [i.e. one day per month of unpaid labor for public
service projects] [...] Just as authorities began the violence,
so they could stop it. In Kibirira they sent two policemen
who halted the killings just by blowing their whistles and
giving the order to disperse.*

(Human Rights Watch in Uvin 1998, 214)

THE RWANDAN STATE

A great deal has been written to explain the genocide in Rwanda.
Like most major historical events—such as wars, revolutions, the
emergence of democracies, and the establishment of dictator-
ships—genocides, too, have varied and complex causes. Single-cause
explanations tend to be overly simplistic and erroneous, as reality is
nearly always much more complex. The genocide in Rwanda can be
explained through a wide spectrum of factors: historical, cultural,
ideological and political, economic and class-oriented, ethnic and

---

[1]   Rwandan lawyer.

demographic. The following subsections will explore the major factors that contributed to the genocide.

The traditional state of Rwanda never had to cope with mass killings or genocide, and there is no doubt that colonialism and postcolonial politics contributed to its decline into the abyss of genocide. Nonetheless, in order to understand the widespread compliance with orders "from above" to kill, and nearly everyone's toeing the line, one must be aware of the country's precolonial political traditions.

For hundreds of years, all Rwandans—Hutu, Tutsi, and Twa—had been accustomed to a centralized authoritarian regime that was obeyed unconditionally. This heritage was manifested on a daily basis as the obligation of *umuganda*, or public community service. From this perspective, Rwanda did not change during the colonial period, as the traditional state remained intact under the system of indirect rule. Indeed, there was continuity between precolonial and postcolonial Rwanda, even though it took the form of a "Hutu republic" and not a Tutsi-ruled monarchy. Like the precolonial and the colonial state, the postcolonial state was hierarchical and centralized. It was also totalitarian in that its institutions penetrated all aspects of the lives of its citizens.

The age-old authoritarian character of the Rwandan state hence explains the efficient operation of the mass-killing apparatus (just as the German-Prussian bureaucratic tradition helps explain the systematic extermination of the Jews of Europe). Rwanda of 1994 was a totalitarian state built on a hierarchy of institutions, down to relatively small cells (*Nyumba Kumi*), with the higher echelons giving orders to kill the Tutsi and moderate Hutu, and the lower echelons obeying orders—as was the tradition (Pottier 2002, 31).

RACIST IDEOLOGY

*The designation of inferior groups comes from those on
top—an expression of their right to rule—as well as from
frustrated persons often near the bottom, as an expression
of their need for security.*

(Simpson and Yinger 1985, 45)

Any attempt to understand the genocide in Rwanda must address
the dimension of ideology. The racist ideology that was dissem-
inated throughout the country in various ways—in books, newspapers, radio broadcasts, community meetings, political speeches,
official documents, churches, and schools—seeped into all parts of
Hutu society. The result was an atmosphere that contributed to the
climate of mass killing.

In the late 1950s and early 1960s, the Hutu had already come to
view the Tutsi as a foreign element with a different bloodline and a
different anatomy from that of the Hutu—"Hamites," who did not
originally stem from the country. They were portrayed as a people
with very different physical traits and racial origins, and a different
history. The Hutu regarded themselves as the legitimate inhabitants
of the country and the Tutsi as foreign Hamites in a land not their
own, and probably stemming from Ethiopia. In addition, the Tutsi
were also portrayed as rich and exploitative tyrants, who had ruled
the country in the past and were now trying to turn back the wheels
of time. Repeated references were made to the "Hamitic threat" and
the "Hamitic conspiracy" (Lemarchand 1996, 95).

It should be noted that this dynamic evolved on the basis of a new
racist discourse according to which the "foreign" Tutsi were inferior
and the Hutu superior, thereby putting the colonial racial theory—
which had justified the nature of Tutsi rule by presenting the light-
skinned Tutsi conquerors as Hamites and superior, and the Bantu
(Hutu) as inferior—on its head. Contrary to this, Hutu racist ideology in postcolonial Rwanda referred to the Tutsi as "cockroaches"
that must be "purged" and "cleansed," a terminology reminiscent of
Nazi Germany. The Hutu thus became the "supreme race," endowed
with a distorted sense of dignity, hope, and glory (Uvin 1998, 98).

Treatment of the Tutsi was not shaped by prevalent moral codes regulating interpersonal behavior, since they were in a sense expelled from Rwandan society.

Accordingly, in the early 1990s, Rwandan Hutu increasingly asserted that the "Tutsi problem" could only be solved by means of a "final solution." This could have taken the form of expulsion, or what was then referred to as "ethnic cleansing."[2] Infinitely worse was the proposed option of extermination. Professor Léon Mugesera of the RTLMC radio station held that the Tutsi needed to be "sent back home to Ethiopia," *via* the Nyabarongo River—into which tens of thousands of murdered Tutsi were thrown in 1994 (Hintjens 1999, 255).

Like in Nazi and other racist ideologies, racism in Rwanda, too, took on a sexual dimension. In precolonial and colonial times, Hutu hatred for the Tutsi was justified by the claim that Tutsi lords took wives from among the Hutu, provoking the hatred of Hutu men. In postcolonial Rwanda, the tables were turned, and members of the Hutu elite married attractive, wealthy Tutsi women, resulting in hatred against these women for "seducing" Hutu men. It was generally assumed that these marriages were part of the "Tutsi conspiracy," and that, when the time came, the Tutsi women would kill their Hutu husbands. In this way, while mixed marriages in Rwanda had been seen as acts of Rwandan integrative patriotism in the past, in the 1980s opposition to such marriages to "foreigners" and "traitors" was on the increase.

The racist ideology was translated into actions from "above" and from "below." From above, it provided ideological legitimacy for discrimination against and oppression of the Tutsi, or even for anti-Tutsi mob attacks and killings. From below, it provided the Hutu, who themselves were poor and persecuted, with a scapegoat that could be blamed for their poverty and frustration.

---

[2] The term "ethnic cleansing," which took root in the 1990s during the war in the Balkans, refers to the expulsion of ethnic groups from a particular region with the aim of ensuring that region for a rival group. Under international law, ethnic cleansing is a crime against humanity.

Illustration 10: "I survived three massacres. I am no longer frightened of death."

If I must die, I will die here. I have nothing left to live for. My grandchildren keep me alive. If my daughter and I must die, I would rather they not save us. It's too difficult. When my grandchild draws soldiers shooting in all directions, I know that if he sees a weapon, he will know how to use it. (Frida, Aged 76; only one of her eight daughters survived)

Explain the "racial logic" of the Hutu Ten Commandments. How do they benefit the Hutu?

The following is a racist text published in the newspaper Kangura in December 1990. The so-called Hutu Ten Commandments became part of an extremist racist worldview.

1. Every Hutu should know that a Tutsi woman, whoever she is, works for the interest of her Tutsi ethnic group. As a result, we shall consider a traitor any Hutu who

   - marries a Tutsi woman

   - befriends a Tutsi woman

   - employs a Tutsi woman as a secretary or a concubine.

2. Every Hutu should know that our Hutu daughters are more suitable and conscientious in their role as woman, wife and mother of the family. Are they not beautiful, good secretaries and more honest?

3. Hutu women, be vigilant and try to bring your husbands, brothers and sons back to reason.

4. Every Hutu should know that every Tutsi is dishonest in business. His only aim is the supremacy of his ethnic group. As a result, any Hutu who does the following is a traitor:

   - makes a partnership with Tutsi in business

   - invests his money or the government's money in a Tutsi enterprise

   - lends or borrows money from a Tutsi

   - gives favours to Tutsi in business (obtaining import licenses, bank loans, construction sites, public markets, etc.).

5. All strategic positions, political, administrative, economic, military and security should be entrusted only to Hutu.

6. The education sector (school pupils, students, teachers) must be majority Hutu.

7. The Rwandan Armed Forces should be exclusively Hutu. The experience of the October 1990 war has taught us a lesson. No member of the military shall marry a Tutsi.

8. The Hutu should stop having mercy on the Tutsi.

9. The Hutu, wherever they are, must have unity and solidarity and be concerned with the fate of their Hutu brothers.

   • The Hutu inside and outside Rwanda must constantly look for friends and allies for the Hutu cause, starting with their Hutu brothers.

   • They must constantly counteract Tutsi propaganda.

   • The Hutu must be firm and vigilant against their common Tutsi enemy.

10. The Social Revolution of 1959, the Referendum of 1961, and the Hutu Ideology, must be taught to every Hutu at every level. Every Hutu must spread this ideology widely. Any Hutu who persecutes his brother Hutu for having read, spread, and taught this ideology is a traitor.

(Berry and Berry 1999, 113–115)

Clarify the meaning of the concepts "racism from above" and "racism from below."

ECONOMIC AND SOCIAL FACTORS

*The people whose children had to walk barefoot to school
killed the people who could buy shoes for theirs. A survivor.*

(Prunier 1995, 250)

*Rwanda was the most densely populated country in
Africa, with one of the world's highest population growth
rates, one of the lowest amounts of arable land per person.*

(Uvin 1998, 181)

In the 1990s, Rwanda was an oppressed and destitute country. An estimated 50% of the population was classified as exceptionally poor (to the point of malnutrition), 40% as poor, 9% as not poor, and 1% as wealthy ("bigmen"). According to US Aid estimates at the time, 90% of the country's agricultural population (accounting for 80% of the total population) was living below the poverty line.

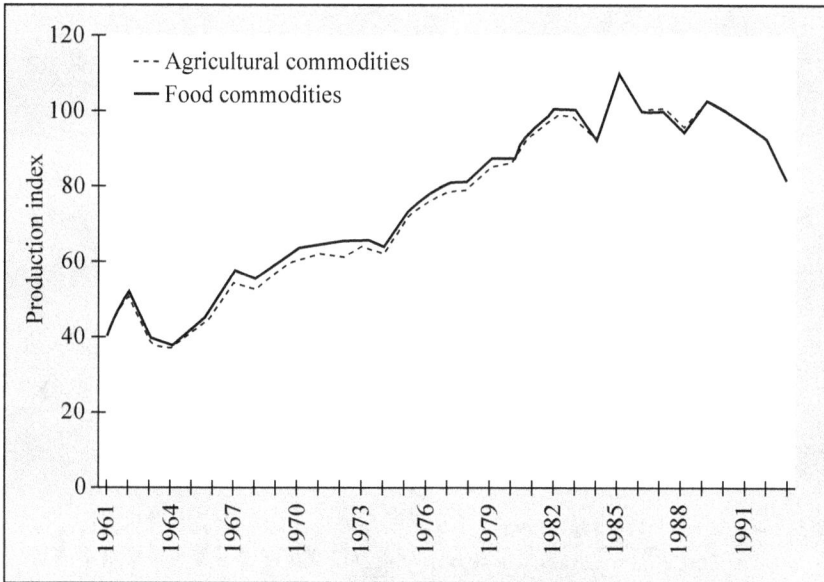

Figure 8: Production of food and agricultural products in Rwanda, 1961–1991 (FAO online data)

The economic crisis of the 1980s further widened the class divisions, increasing corruption among the country's elite and impoverishing the farming population even more (Uvin 1998, 117).

The economic data for Rwanda during these years illustrate the depth of the economic crisis. Whereas Rwanda's annual per capita GNP in 1976 was higher than that of the neighboring countries, by 1990 it had dropped below that of all its neighbors (Mamdani 2001, 144). The annual per capita GNP plummeted from $355 in 1983, to $330 in 1989, to $260 in 1990, and to $200 in 1993 (Guichaoua 1995, 33).

In the 1980s, annual economic growth stood at 1.3%, while agricultural production grew at an even slower rate of 0.3%.

During these years, Rwanda's population grew by 3.3% per annum, resulting in a steady decrease in per capita GNP and agricultural produce. In the early 1990s, economic growth in the country was negative. The daily number of calories consumed per person dropped from 2,055 in 1984 to 1,509 in 1991 (Uvin 1998, 54, 98).

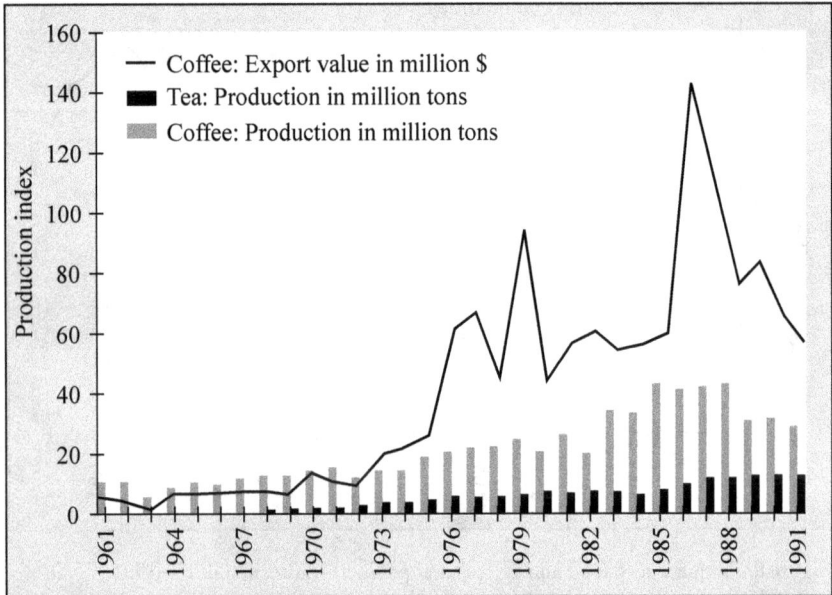

Figure 9: Coffee and tea production and exports in Rwanda, 1961–1991 (FAO online)

The Rwandan economy suffered tremendously from the steep drop in income from exports. For example, falling world coffee prices, together with the spread of a forest disease that resulted in the uprooting of 300,000 trees, caused coffee exports to drop from $144 million per year in 1985 to $30 million per year in 1993. The prices of tea and tin, Rwanda's other major exports, also dropped steadily. Concurrently, the country's national debt increased from $189 million in 1980 to $941 million in 1993.

An attempt by the World Bank and the International Monetary Fund in 1991 to stabilize the Rwandan economy by means of a Structural Adjustment Program (SAP) was unsuccessful. The policy of privatization, the slashing of subsidies, and the shrinking of the public administration resulted in a steep increase in food and water prices and a 40% cutback in the educational and health services in the country. The result was mass famine that plagued southern Rwanda in 1989—the country's first famine since 1943.

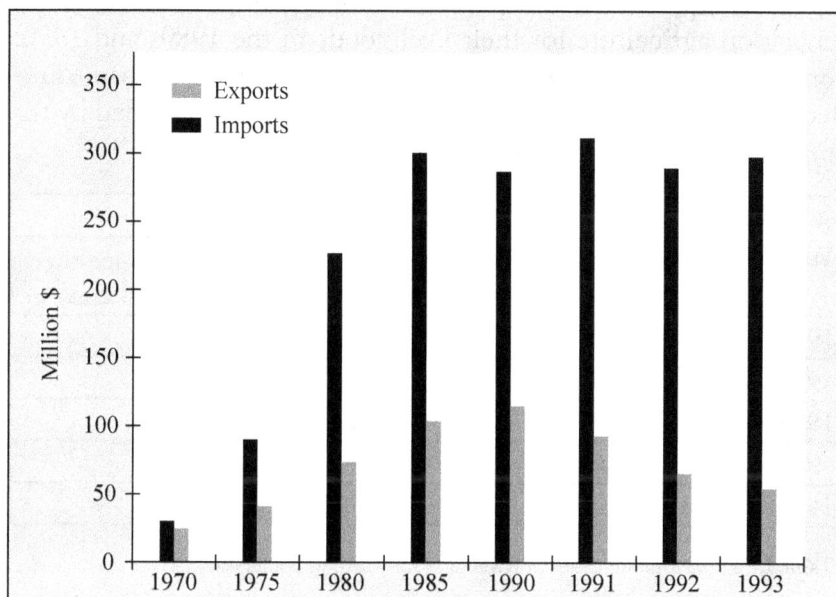

Figure 10: Overall exports and imports in Rwanda, 1970–1993 (UN Statistical Yearbook for Africa)

Another cause of the economic decline was the war between the government and RPF, which resulted in a sharp expansion of the military on the one hand (from 7,000 men in 1990 to 50,000 men in 1994), and major expenditures for a massive purchase of weapons on the other (40% of the national budget was redirected to defence and war expenditures). By October 1990, a mass flight of refugees was underway on the northern front. This not only meant that the north ceased to function as a productive economic region; it also meant that the central region was now forced to resettle the many refugees.

The state of the economy brought about widespread starvation amongst the farmers, while the decline in exports and reduction in foreign aid also dealt a serious blow to the country's elites. The combination of a destitute and hungry populace and an impoverished socioeconomic elite is always lethal because it creates pressure from "below" and willingness from "above" to adopt solutions that may seem simple and effective, but are in fact misleading, aggressive, and often even brutal.

One major problem caused by the economic turmoil and the widening social gaps was the land problem: although the number of people relying on agriculture for their livelihoods in the 1980s and 1990s continued to increase, the peasants continued to share the same limited area of agricultural land. This problem was compounded by the country's high population density (see Table 12).

Year	Population Data		
	Total Population	Population per km^2	Population per km^2 (agricultural area)
1934	1,595,000	61	85
1950	1,954,000	73	102
1970	3,756,000	143	200
1980	5,257,000	200	281
1989	7,128,000	270	380

Table 13: Population densities in Rwanda, 1934–1989 (Prunier 1996, 4)

Over the years, the land plots allocated to each family (see Table 13) became smaller, and the land itself became less and less fertile as a result of overuse. At the same time, the population increased significantly (in 1994, 60% of the Rwandan population was under the age of 20). Indeed, Thomas Malthus's vision of a so-called solution to the problem of overpopulation, namely famine and war, was actualized in Rwanda.3 However, in the Rwandan case, in addition to famine and war, there was also genocide.

---

3   Thomas Robert Malthus (1766–1834) was a British economist, Anglican clergyman, and professor of history; he was well-known primarily for his "Essay on the Principle of Population and its Future Influence on Society" (1798). In his essay, Malthus developed what was to become known as the "Malthusian Law," which maintains that human population increases exponentially as a result of natural reproduction, while agricultural output increases arithmetically at best. According to Malthus, balance between natural reproduction and increased means of subsistence can be achieved only through "internal" intervention (abortions and birthrate planning) or "external" intervention (wars, epidemics, and famines). Most of Malthus's conjectures were proven to be incorrect.

In any event, the wide class disparities took the form of ethnic tensions, resulting in spontaneous acts of murder. Elegantly dressed people or people carrying large bags were murdered on the city streets, as were car owners or people who spoke French. The assumption was that they were wealthy Tutsi (in fact, Hutu were sometimes killed by mistake, as the murderers were not overly concerned with "mere" facts).

Year	Area
1949	3 hectares (1 hectare ≈ 2.5 acres)
1960	2 hectares
1980	1.2 hectares
1990	0.7 hectares

Table 14: Average area of the family farm in Rwanda (Uvin 1998, 188)

Later, members of the Hutu *Lumpenproletariat*—unemployed people, ruffians, and thieves—became more prominent in the militias. It should be noted that these militiamen were also motivated by greed and were permitted to ransack shops, loot, or even to seize control of lands, fields and homes.

In this context, the genocide in Rwanda can be regarded as a typical expression of "structured violence:" violence stemming from wide structural and socioeconomic intergroup disparities and from the feeling that the inequality is a product of injustice, discrimination, and exploitation — both historical and contemporary. In general, tensions in situations like these are easily manipulated by demagogy and incitement from above, causing people to direct their anger at the wealthy—whether that wealth is real or imagined (Adelman 2000, 435).

Against the background of such deep economic problems, Rwanda's social tensions were felt even more strongly. As we have seen, urban Tutsi were more successful from a socioeconomic perspective than urban Hutu. They were more conspicuous among university graduates and the free professions, among business owners, and, for example, among employees of foreign embassies. However, the perception of Tutsi as wealthy was based on an assessment of the urban elite alone. The Tutsi living in the villages were often poor farmers and cattle owners, known as "small Tutsis."

Give examples of other instances in which an economic crisis served as an impetus for genocide.

THE WAR AND THE GENOCIDE

War provides cover for rulers to carry out projects of ethnic cleansing.

(Naimark 2002, 187)

It is impossible to explain the genocide in Rwanda without addressing its wartime context. The same holds for the many other cases of genocide that took place during wars, conquest and occupation, or the suppression of rebellions. These include the Holocaust, the genocide in Cambodia, the murder of the Native Americans of North America, the conquests of Genghis Kahn, and the killing of the Herero people of German South-West Africa (today's Namibia).

The Hutu war against the Tutsi guerilla movement, which began in October 1990, provides part of the explanation for the Rwandan genocide three-and-a-half years later. The Hutu suffered heavy casualties in the northern part of the country and hundreds of thousands fled the advance of the invading forces, fears of which were deep-seated. The war made it easier for the regime to disseminate its racist ideology, unite the Hutu camp (in part through a split in the opposition parties), and demand unquestioning obedience to the authorities. The militarization of Rwandan society resulted in the formation of hundreds of "security associations" and "death squads." Scores of Rwandan Hutu joined the militias, and acts of murder were always justified as actions against the "enemies," the "traitors," the "fifth column," or the "collaborators." Ultimately, this process culminated in the legitimization of the genocide (see Figure 11).

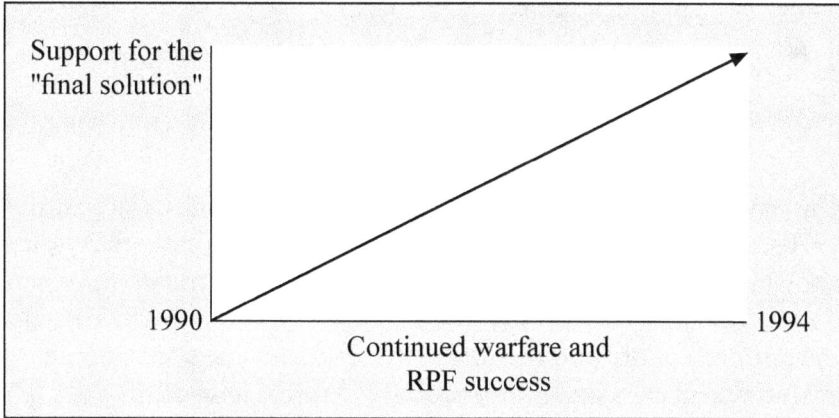

Figure 11: Wartime threat and support for genocide

Some argue that the killing of the Tutsi was an "act of war." Why is this claim illegitimate and immoral?

GENOCIDE AND THE ERA OF DEMOCRATIZATION

But this genocide was not an uncontrollable outburst of rage by a people consumed by 'ancient tribal hatreds.' Nor was it the preordained result of the impersonal forces of poverty and over-population. This genocide resulted from the deliberate choice of a modern elite to foster hatred and fear to keep itself in power. This small, privileged group first set the majority against the minority to counter a growing political opposition within Rwanda.

(Des Forges 1999, 1)

If the international community is unwilling to defend the democratic changes it set in motion when they are threatened—the end result may be a much worse situation, as the case of Rwanda shows.

(Uvin 1998, 236)

> *"Democratization" programs—often devised in the*
> *West—need to be rethought; in Rwanda they contributed*
> *to, rather than alleviated, the crisis.*
>
> (Newbury 1995, 17)

This raises the question of why genocide did not take place in the 1970s or the 1980s, when Rwanda was ruled by a single-party dictatorship, but in the 1990s, in the "era of democratization," when Rwanda could lay claim to multiple political parties, a parliamentary opposition, a multi-party coalition that included the opposition parties, and print media that also produced critical journalism.

In the context of Rwanda in the early 1990s, one must understand the critical difference between democracy and democratization. A stable democracy is a regime that ensures the provision of human and civil rights and security for minority groups, and typically redirects towards other outlets what might otherwise have been a violent conflict. In a stable democracy, the democratic regime is the "only game in town." Democratization, on the other hand, is a process intended to help a society navigate from a dissolving dictatorship to a developing a democracy. The democratization process, however, may remain incomplete. Countries undergoing democratization processes frequently encounter periods of instability, often characterized by violence. Such situations are liable to degenerate into massacres, civil wars, and wars between two sovereign states. In the 1990s, this was the case in the former Yugoslavia, Sri Lanka, Kenya, Zimbabwe, and Burundi. It was also the case in Rwanda.

Throughout the democratization process in Rwanda, the tyrannical Hutu regime felt threatened by thriving opposition newspapers that had started to speak out increasingly against the corrupt northern oligarchy and supported the Hutu opposition parties (the MDR, the PL, the PSD, and the PDC), which posed a concrete threat to the regime. The prospect of free elections was a sword of Damocles hanging over the Habyarimana regime. This threat was accentuated by the Arusha Accords, which mandated the establishment of a Broad Based Transitional Government. The MRNDD establishment was faced with the very real possibility of the opposition parties (which supported democracy) joining forces with the RPF in the government and possibly in the coming elections, and of the fall of Habyarimana, the *clan de Madame*, and the racist establishment. The "solution" they found was to incite the Hutu along ethnoracial lines against the opposition parties, which were portrayed as collaborators with the "Tutsi enemy." This eventually led to splits within the opposition parties. At the same time, along with making use of the Tutsi threat, the northern Hutu oligarchy looked to the Hutu masses, including the poor and the southern Hutu, as a force for carrying out the racist murder campaign. The government repeatedly asserted that the democratization that had been forced on it was no more than a code word for Tutsi seizure of power, and declared itself to be the true representative of "real democracy," on the premise that it embodied the rule of the "democratic majority."

Some scholars maintain that external pressure toward democratization by Western countries had the opposite effect; or, in other words, that it was democratization which ultimately brought about the attempt to halt democratization by means of genocide. This dynamic supports the argument according to which pressuring fundamentally antidemocratic rulers to democratize their countries may result in their use of ethnic incitement, ethnic cleansing, and even genocide, in an effort to remain in power. According to many observers, this is what happened in Rwanda (Uvin 1998, 234–235).

BURUNDI

Explaining Rwanda through Burundi.
(Hintjens 1999, 276)

The countries of Rwanda and Burundi can be thought of as Siamese twins: during the precolonial period, each was a traditional kingdom ruled by a Tutsi dynasty with an identical ratio of Hutu majority to Tutsi minority (85% Hutu, 14% Tutsi). Subsequently, both countries were incorporated into the same colonial-governing framework (Rwanda-Urundi), first under German rule (1898–1916) and subsequently under Belgian rule (1918–1962). In both countries, the

Tutsi monarchy remained intact throughout the colonial period, and it was only in 1962 that Rwanda and Urundi (which was renamed Burundi) became separate independent states.

Map 11: Rwanda and Burundi

The 1959 Hutu revolution in Rwanda resulted in major differences between the two countries. Since then, developments in Rwanda have determined the fate of Burundi, and events in Burundi have been essential to understanding the developments in Rwanda.

In response to the Hutu revolution in Rwanda, and the killings and expulsions they involved, a determined Tutsi regime entrenched itself in Burundi. This regime exercised its power against the Hutu in Burundi, who regarded the 1959 revolution in Rwanda as an example to be emulated. In 1966, a military coup in Burundi toppled the royal dynasty and brought to power a group of extremist Tutsi. In this way, Tutsi rule in Burundi continued, despite the demise of the monarchy and its replacement with a republican military regime.

Between 1962 and 1994, the regimes in Rwanda and Burundi were mirror images of each other: in Rwanda, a Hutu regime ruled and oppressed the Tutsi with the aid of an all-Hutu military; in Burundi, a Tutsi regime ruled and oppressed the Hutu with the aid of an all-Tutsi military. Thus, Hutu oppression in Burundi served to justify Tutsi oppression in Rwanda, and vice-versa. In Burundi, developments in Rwanda resulted in widespread fear of the Hutu, and in Rwanda, developments in Burundi resulted in widespread fear of the Tutsi. Every massacre against Hutu in Burundi resulted in anti-Tutsi mob violence in Rwanda. Tens of thousands of Tutsi refugees from Rwanda strengthened the Tutsi regime in Burundi, and hundreds of thousands of Hutu refugees from Burundi radicalized the anti-Tutsi racist policies in Rwanda.

Years	Country		
	Rwanda	**Rwanda-Urundi**	**Burundi**
pre-1898	Tutsi rule	—	Tutsi rule
1898–1916	Tutsi rule	Indirect German rule	Tutsi rule
1918–1962	Tutsi rule	Indirect Belgian rule	Tutsi rule
1962–1994	Hutu rule	—	Tutsi rule
1994–2004	Tutsi rule	—	Tutsi rule

Table 15: The Tutsi and Hutu regimes in Rwanda and Burundi

From time to time, the Hutu in Burundi rebelled against the Tutsi regime, resulting in fierce suppression and massacres of the Hutu population by the Burundi military—most prominently in 1965, 1972, and 1988. In the 1960s and 1970s, Burundi was rocked by the assassination of three prime ministers, a number of government ministers, and all the Hutu members of parliament.

For the Hutu of Rwanda, the failed Hutu rebellion in Burundi in 1972 was particularly traumatic, as the Burundi army killed 150,000 Hutu, including the entire political leadership and intelligentsia. These events caused the extremist Hutu in Rwanda, led by General Habyarimana, to seize power in 1973 and to intensify oppression of the Tutsi.

Due to international pressure for democratization, Pierre Buyoya, Burundi's extremist Tutsi military ruler, agreed to hold the first free elections in the country's history (see Table 15). In the elections, which were held on June 1, 1993, Buyoya ran against moderate Hutu candidate Melchior Ndadaye. Buyoya appears to have believed that manipulation, forgery, falsification, threats, and other forms of pressure would enable him to carry the election. However, to his chagrin, it was Ndadaye who emerged victorious with an overwhelming majority of 64.8%, making him not only Burundi's first democratically elected president, but its first Hutu president as well. After the presidential elections, parliamentary elections were held on June 29, 1993, in which the moderate Hutu party known as the Front for Democracy in Burundi (*Front pour la démocratie au Burundi*), or FRODEBU, won an impressive majority, taking 65 of the 81 seats in parliament.

Regime Institution	Candidate or Party	Ethnic Character	Votes / Seats
Presidency	Melchior Ndadaye	Hutu	64.8%
	Pierre Buyoya	Tutsi	33.0%
National Assembly	FRODEBU	Hutu (moderate leadership)	71.04%
	UPRONA	Tutsi	21.34%

Table 16: The election results in Burundi, June 1993

The establishment of a government with fifteen Hutu and seven Tutsi ministers (including the prime minister, who was a moderate Tutsi) marked the completion of the reversal of power in Burundi.

The rise to power of moderate Hutu in Burundi, the non-violent democratization, and the formation of a mixed government raised hopes among the moderate Hutu of Rwanda, who had fought for coexistence, compromise, and peace within the framework of the Arusha Accords. Their hopes, however, were dealt a mortal blow on October 21, 1993, when Tutsi officers in Burundi assassinated the newly elected president, the speaker of the National Assembly, and three government ministers. As a result, a Hutu rebellion erupted throughout Burundi, which the army put down with an iron fist. The Hutu murdered approximately 20,000 rural Tutsi, and caused another 150,000 Tutsi villagers to flee their homes to the capital, which was then under military control. The army struck at the Hutu, slaughtering 30,000 and causing 400,000 to flee to Rwanda.

The events in Burundi had disastrous effects in Rwanda. The message that became deeply entrenched among the Hutu in Burundi and Rwanda alike after Ndadaye's assassination was "never trust the Tutsi" (Magnarella 2000, 18). The radical Hutu establishment in Rwanda regarded the advance of RPF forces, the Arusha Accords, and the assassination of President Ndadaye in Burundi as part of one great conspiracy aimed at the creation of a Tutsi empire. In light of the developments, Rwandan President Habyarimana resolved not to implement the Arusha Accords, and the radicals in the MRNDD, the CDR, the militias, and the security forces reached the conclusion that their only choice was a "final solution": the extermination of all Tutsi. From a Hutu perspective, the Tutsi in Burundi had proven their treachery and shown that Tutsi would never truly accept Hutu majority rule. The Hutu in Rwanda were convinced that there could never be a political agreement with the RPF, not to mention integration of the Hutu Rwandan army and the mainly Tutsi RPF forces.

The killing also sparked a marked radicalization of the more moderate Hutu. Majorities within the liberal democratic opposition parties of the MDR and the PL (and minorities within the PSD and the PDC) now joined the racist radical front known as Hutu Power. At the same time, masses of revenge-seeking Hutu refugees from

Burundi joined the murderous militias. In brief, it was no doubt the October 1993 killing in Burundi that sparked the massive eruption that rocked Rwanda in April 1994.

6

PUNISHING THE *GÉNOCIDAIRES*

*If South Africa exemplifies the dilemma involved in
the pursuit of reconciliation without justice, Rwanda
exemplifies the opposite: the pursuit of justice without
reconciliation.*

(Mamdani 1996, 4)

German philosopher Karl Jaspers identified four concepts of guilt in
the context of post-World War II Germany: *criminal guilt*, borne by
the murderers themselves; *political guilt*, borne by the entire citizenry
of a modern state; *moral guilt* of those who were "only" carrying
out orders; and *metaphysical guilt* of those who remained passive
and failed to prevent injustice and crimes (Jaspers 1948, 25–26).
This chapter does not purport to discuss collective punishment, the
denunciation of a passive population in an indifferent world, or the
denunciation of evil in general; rather, it focuses on the culpability
or, to be more precise, the punishment of individual perpetrators.

Punishment of the perpetrators of the Rwanda genocide was han-
dled by two institutions: the International Criminal Tribunal for
Rwanda, which was established in Arusha, Tanzania especially for
this purpose; and the local Rwandan courts. At a later date, another
possibility emerged, namely that of trying the murderers in the
courts of other countries.

The International Criminal Tribunal for Rwanda (ICTR) was
established by the UN Security Council in Resolution 955 (dated
November 8, 1994), in accordance with its authority under Chapter VII of the United Nations Charter on "Action with Respect to
Threats to the Peace, Breaches of the Peace, and Acts of Aggression."
Resolution 955, it should be emphasized, did not limit ICTR jurisdiction to the crimes committed by one side alone. The Tribunal was
given "the power to prosecute persons responsible for serious violations of international humanitarian law committed in the territory

of Rwanda and by Rwandan citizens in the territory of neighboring states between January 1, 1994 and December 31, 1994;" that is to say that the ICTR could also try members of the RPF. The tribunal, it was decided, would try all those responsible for genocide, crimes against humanity,[1] and war crimes, and would impose penalties "limited to imprisonment." The resolution was supported by thirteen members of the Security Council and opposed by the representative of the new Rwandan government (which disagreed with the decision to refrain from using the death penalty, with location of the tribunal outside Rwanda, and with its jurisdiction restricted to crimes committed after to April 6, 1994). Only one country, namely China, abstained.

In contrast to the Rwandan courts, and in contrast to the International Military Tribunal at Nuremberg (or the Nuremberg Trials) and the International Military Tribunal for the Far East (or the Tokyo War Crimes Tribunal), both of which operated after World War II, the ICTR would not be authorized to issue the death penalty (in accordance with the International Covenant on Civil and Political Rights). Paradoxically, then, the major criminals tried by the International Tribunal would be exempt from the death penalty, while "lesser" murderers tried before the local courts in Rwanda could be sentenced to death.

It was also determined that the International Tribunal would enjoy primacy over the local Rwandan courts, meaning that a murderer held in a Rwandan jail but required for proceedings before the International Tribunal could be extradited for that purpose (and in this way could escape the death penalty). This rule was also applicable to defendants whose trials in Rwanda were already under way. Moreover, a person who had already been tried in Rwanda could, under certain circumstances, be retried by the International Tribunal, but not vice versa.

According to Article 6 ("Individual criminal responsibility") of the Statute of the Tribunal, commanders could be tried for orders they issued, but soldiers who killed could not use such orders in their own

---

[1]   The concept "crimes against humanity" was first used in court against Nazi leaders during the Nuremberg Trials.

defence (as such orders are regarded as "blatantly illegal" in international law).

The Security Council also resolved that UN member countries had to consent to requests for the extradition of suspects. Countries that arrested and extradited suspects included Belgium, Switzerland, the United States, and a number of countries in Africa (Burkina Faso, Cameroon, Kenya, Ivory Coast, Mali, Togo, Zambia, and Tanzania).

As proscribed by the 1994 Security Council Resolution, which was amended over the years, the ICTR consisted of four chambers: three trial chambers, located in Arusha, Tanzania (unlike the tribunals in Nuremberg and Tokyo, which were established in the countries in which the crimes were committed), and an appeals chamber (which also serves as the appeals chamber for the International Criminal Tribunal for former Yugoslavia) located in The Hague, Netherlands. The office of the deputy prosecutor and his staff was established in Kigali, because investigations had to be carried out in Rwanda. The latest revised ICTR Statutes (2010) appear in their entirety in Appendix 3.

THE INTERNATIONAL CRIMINAL TRIBUNAL FOR RWANDA

It was decided that rulings of the ICTR would be based on a majority and that tribunal employees (a staff of approximately 800, including judges, investigators, and administrative workers) would be guarded by UN forces (UNAMIR). Of the first six judges elected by the UN General Assembly, three were African. The president of the first tribunal was Laity Kama of Senegal, and the first chief prosecutor was South African supreme court justice Richard Goldstone, who also served as the prosecutor for the International Criminal Tribunal for former Yugoslavia. In 1996, Goldstone was replaced by Canadian judge Louise Arbour.

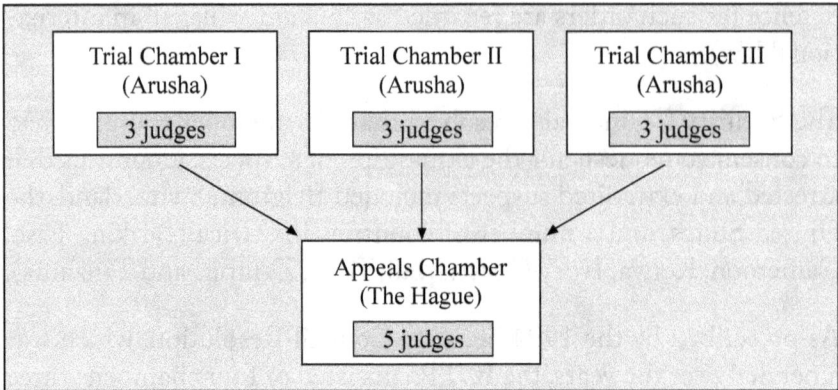

Figure 12: Structure of the International Criminal Tribunal for Rwanda

By March 2011, the work of the tribunal had resulted in the arrest of 81 *génocidaires*, 38 of whom were convicted. These included, amongst others, former Rwandan prime minister Jean Kambanda (see details below), RTLMC director Ferdinand Nahimana, and *Kangura* editor Hassan Ngeze (in December 2003, both were sentenced to life imprisonment). Ten individuals who were indicted are still at large, including Augustin Bizimana, minister of defence in the Interim Government. Major genocide instigator Théoneste Bagosora was extradited to the Arusha Tribunal in 1997; in December 2008, he was found guilty and sentenced to life imprisonment (later reduced to thirty-five years imprisonment).

The Trial of Jean Kambanda
(Magnarella 2000, 85–93)

In 1994, Jean Kambanda, Rwanda's racist prime minister at the time of the genocide, was thirty-nine years of age, married with two children, and a trained engineer, who had formerly worked as a bank manager. A leader of the extremist wing of the MDR, Kambanda was the natural heir to Prime Minister Agathe Uwilingiyamana, leader of the moderate wing of the MDR who, as we have noted, was murdered at the outset of the genocide. During the massacres, Kambanda could be seen on television screens round the country distributing machetes to militia members. In a well-known radio broadcast from the period, Kambanda called on

Tutsis to leave their hiding places because "the war has ended," a call intended to reveal the whereabouts of additional Tutsis with the aim of killing them .

After the genocide, Kambanda fled to Zaire and, from there, to Kenya, where he was detained and surrendered to the Tribunal in Arusha after the exertion of massive pressure by the Tribunal itself. He was charged with genocide, conspiracy to commit genocide, incitement to commit genocide, complicity in genocide, and crimes against humanity (murder).

Throwing himself at the mercy of the court, he confessed to the following charges:

- Participating in the cabinet and Council of Minister meetings that discussed the genocide.
- Involvement in the dismissal of the prefect of Butare, who refused to carry out orders to commit genocide.
- Conducting meetings with army leaders to coordinate the war against the RPF "partners" (meaning, the Tutsi civilian population).
- Making media appearances to mobilize the general population to massacre Tutsis.
- Making "field visits" to encourage the general population to carry out killings.
- Inciting prefects and commune managers to organize the killings in the communes.
- Witnessing murders.

The court accepted Kambanda's confession but did not lighten his sentence. The defendant's confession, the Tribunal determined, was not a reflection of regret or empathy for the victims, or a justification for his actions. In September 1998, Kambanda was sentenced to a maximum life sentence.

The trials of the ICTR were the first genocide trials in history (the Nuremberg Trials and the Tokyo Trials tried German and Japanese officials for crimes against peace, crimes against humanity, and war crimes—but not genocide). It is also notable that the ICTR trials were the first in history to recognize rape as a component of genocide and of crimes against humanity, in accordance with the Convention on the Prevention and Punishment of the Crime of Genocide (Crampton 2001; Magnarella 2000).

THE LOCAL COURTS IN RWANDA

As noted, the Tribunal in Arusha tried the "big fish," while the cases of other murderers were adjudicated by the Rwandan courts. According to estimates, some 300,000 people were involved in the murders. Of these, an estimated 130,000 suspects were still imprisoned in Rwanda in 2001 (in prisons with a capacity of 12,000).

Rwandan law distinguishes between four categories of people that can be tried for their actions in 1994:

- Those who planned, organized, incited, supervised, and led the genocide and the crimes against humanity. This category includes all those who held key positions in the government, the army, and the militias, the parties, and the churches, as well as particularly brutal murderers.
- Murderers and accessories to murder.
- Suspects charged with raping and injuring others.
- Suspects charged with destruction of property.

Under Rwandan law, it is only permissible (though not mandatory) to impose the death penalty on members of the first group.

The Rwandan legal system faced monumental difficulties. Of the 1,000 judges serving in the courts in April 1994, only 100 remained in Rwanda after the genocide, and of the country's 100 prosecutors, only 12 remained. Most of the missing judges and prosecutors were Hutu who fled Rwanda in fear of revenge after the RPF victory; in point of fact, some Tutsi and moderate Hutu judges and prosecutors were killed during the genocide. Finding lawyers to defend the accused also presented a major challenge, as many members of the legal profession refused to defend murderers for ethical reasons, or in order to avoid the harassment they feared would ensue.

Illustration 11: "But at night we are alone, and then it all comes back"

My first problem is to find food. I am constantly thinking of my three children who were murdered in the genocide. I still have three daughters, ages ten, sixteen, and eighteen. I try to explain to them that they must go to school in order to find work.

My daughters ask me: Why should we work? Will we be able to live? Is it worth it? Is it worth living? I don't know what to tell them. I feel the same way.

There is one thing of which I am certain—that I will die soon, because the people they put in prison think that the widows testified against them and are responsible for their imprisonment. Most of the men died. I do not know the people who killed my family. I fled relatively quickly. I know that if they are released, as tends to happen, they will try to catch us. I try to shake off these disturbing thoughts. During the day it is hard, but work enables us to preoccupy ourselves with other things from time to time. But at night we are alone, and then it all comes back. (Immaculee, Aged 56)

The legal proceedings in Rwanda moved forward at an extremely slow pace. By 1998, the regular courts had managed to try a mere 5,000 out of the tens of thousands of suspects overcrowding the jails. Of these, 400 received the death sentence, while another 500 were acquitted of all charges. Twenty-two of those convicted of genocide were executed by firing squad in April 1998. Below is a description of the trial of a political leader, Froduald Karamira, conducted in a Rwandan court (Magnarella 2000, 279–280).

The Trial of Froduald Karamira

Froduald Karamira, a Rwandan businessman and political leader, he drove around in his Mercedes Benz during the genocide, flanked by soldiers and repeatedly killing Tutsis who had been stopped at checkpoints. His calls for the murder of Tutsis were broadcast daily on the radio.

It is interesting to note that Karamira himself had Tutsi origins, and had been arrested for six months in October 1990 on charges of "collaborating" with the RPF. He later claimed that he was not a Tutsi, emphasizing his claims by acting like a radical Hutu. Karamira was a leader of the racist wing of the MDR (which became known as Hutu Power).

After the victory of the RPF, Karamira fled to India, whence he was extradited back to Rwanda. He escaped during a stopover in Ethiopia, but he was again apprehended, this time by the Ethiopians. Karamira's arrest resulted in a confrontation between the Rwandan government and the international tribunal, each demanding his extradition into its own custody. After the intervention of the president of Rwanda, the Ethiopian authorities resolved to extradite him to Rwanda (in contravention of the ICTR statute).

During his trial (which included the testimony of a man whose wife, mother, four sisters, two cousins, and five children were murdered under Karamira's orders), he expressed no remorse and claimed that it had not been a case of genocide, but rather spontaneous mutual killing.

Karamira was sentenced to be executed by firing squad. Although the pope, the European Union, and the United States all intervened in an effort to prevent his execution, Karamira's sentence was carried out on April 25, 1998.

In 2000, to lighten the case load of the Rwandan courts, it was decided to gradually release elderly defendants and defendants suffering from illnesses, as well as those who were still minors at the time the murders were committed. In 2001, in an effort to contend with the problem of overcrowded prisons and the slow judicial process of the conventional courts, it was decided to set up thousands of traditional popular courts presided over by judges who were selected at village meetings and received six months of legal training. To bring about national reconciliation, these courts were supposed to operate according to Rwanda's traditional *gacaca* system, based on a public confession of guilt and expression of contrition by the accused. Between 2003 and 2010, the *gacaca* courts actually released tens of thousands of murderers. Without a doubt, Rwanda clearly tried to learn from the successful experience of South Africa's establishment of the Truth and Reconciliation Commission (which operated in a similar manner after the collapse of the Apartheid regime).[2]

As noted above, in addition to the International tribunal and the *gacaca* courts, an additional option for bringing the perpetrators to justice were local courts in other countries. A typical example would be the trial of former Rwandan mayor Fulgence Niyontese, who had been charged with ordering the murder and kidnapping of Tutsi and with misusing a meeting in his town to incite Hutu to kill their

---

[2] The Truth and Reconciliation Commission was established in South Africa in 1995, after the transition to black majority rule under the leadership of Nelson Mandela. The commission was chaired by Nobel Peace Prize recipient Bishop Desmond Tutu. The aim of the commission was to verify the facts of the crimes committed by both the government and its opponents during the struggle against Apartheid. Anyone who testified truthfully was assured immunity from prosecution, even if he or she confessed to having committed acts of murder or even massacres. Proponents of the idea regarded it as a significant step toward reconciliation between whites and blacks. In this way, officials of the white regime and the South African security forces, as well as members of the African National Congress and other African movements were able to testify and confess to crimes such as murder, massacre, and torture without being punished. Those who refused to acknowledge their crimes were not granted immunity.

Tutsi neighbors, by a Swiss military tribunal in 1999 (Magnarella 2000, 93).

A Belgian law enacted in 1999 actually facilitated the trial of any person—regardless of citizenship—for war crimes or crimes against humanity committed in another country. This law made possible the 2001 trial of a group of defendants known as the "Butare four," whose members are described below:[3]

- Dr. Alphonse Higaniro, a businessman and former government minister, owner of a match factory, and mathematics graduate of the University of Louvain in Belgium. Higaniro, who was also the son-in-law of Habyarimana's personal physician, bankrolled the *Interahamwe* and transformed his factory into a training base for the vicious militias. Among other things, Higaniro issued orders to "clean" his factory (of Tutsi) and to complete the " 'job' (i.e. the killing) [...] for the sake of the security of Butare" At his trial, the defendant maintained that the instructions he issued had been in reference to the need to clean the factory of a stream of mud in the parking lot. However, he was unable to explain how this would further "the security of Butare," and why the words "clean" and "job" appeared in quotation marks in the instructions he issued. Higaniro was convicted and sentenced to twenty years in prison.

- Physics professor Vincent Ntezimana of the National University of Rwanda, also a graduate of the University of Louvain (to which he returned to teach after the genocide), was tried for compiling lists of university lecturers that were to be murdered, and for personally murdering at least one of his colleagues. He was sentenced to twelve years in prison.

- Benedictine nun Consolata Mukangango ("Sister Gertrude") from the Sovu Convent was tried for delivering 7,000 Tutsi into the hands of murderers on April 22, 1994, for running over dying Tutsi with her car, for handing over relatives of Tutsi nuns who had been in hiding in the convent (and whom the murderers somehow had not harmed), and for insisting on the "evacuation" of the last remaining Tutsi hiding in the convent in a letter to the mayor, dated May 5, 1994. In her own defense, Sister Gertrude maintained that her actions had been intended "to save the convent." She was sentenced to five years in prison.

---

3   For more on this topic, see Aviva Aviram, "The Bigwig, the Intellectual, and the Two Nuns," *Ha'aretz* (June 18, 2001) [Hebrew].

- Julienne Mukabutera ("Sister Kizito"), another nun from the Sovu convent, was charged with supplying the gasoline used to burn alive 500 Tutsi locked in the garage of the convent's health clinic, and with walking among the bodies of the dead Tutsi, cursing them for having torn their paper currency before their death. She was sentenced to twelve years in prison.

Compare and contrast the three legal bodies engaged in punishing the perpetrators of the Rwandan genocide.

7

AFTER THE GENOCIDE: THE NEW RWANDA

The only peace possible between Tutsi and Hutu is an armed peace.

(Mamdani 2001, 271)

Never again.[1]

(Mamdani 2001, 271)

In the months following the genocide, Rwanda experienced migration on an unprecedented scale. Hundreds of thousands of Tutsi returned to the country from their exile in Uganda, Tanzania, and Burundi, while at the same time approximately two million Hutu left the country, mostly for Zaire (later renamed Democratic Republic of Congo, or DRC), though some also made their way to Tanzania and Burundi. Many Hutu returned to Rwanda from late 1994 onwards, but hundreds of thousands (including numerous murderers) remained in refugee camps in Congo and Tanzania. As in April–June 1994, when many Hutu took possession of the homes and fields of murdered Tutsi, so did returning Tutsi now take possession of the homes and fields of absent Hutu who had fled for their lives.

All in all, 900,000 people were murdered in a mere three months. Yet the RPF ultimately won the war. On July 5, 1994, its forces occupied Kigali, and by July 15 it had regained control of the entire country, except for the "safe humanitarian zone," which it eventually occupied upon the withdrawal of French forces, on August 22, 1994.

In the wake of its victory, the RPF set up a coalition government with the liberal-democratic wings of the opposition parties (the MDR, the PSD, the PL, and the PDC), but excluding the MRNDD. Pas-

---

[1]   A common motto among the Tutsi.

teur Bizimungu, a Hutu member of the RPF, was selected to serve as president, and Faustin Twagiramungu, a Hutu of the MDR party, became the new prime minister. Most cabinet ministers of the newly established government were also Hutu. The ethnic composition of the new governing elite constituted a clear statement by the RPF that Rwanda would not be placed under purely Tutsi rule. This approach was consistent with RPF ideology, which held that there was only "one Rwandan people," and that the distinction between Hutu and Tutsi was devoid of historical foundation and was nothing more than a racist colonial "invention." Pottier speaks about the myth of an ancient, unified "true nation" (Pottier 2002, 116). This ideology led to the outlawing of ethnicity and the prohibition of ethnic parties, and became legally binding in the 2003 constitution. The constitution banned any party that "threatens national unity" or "identifies itself with a race, ethnic group, a tribe, a clan, a region, a sex, a religion or any other element that could serve as a basis for discrimination" (*Africa Confidential*, 13 June 2003). The constitution sanctioned, and still does so, any party that represented national unity and reflected that unity in the mobilization of its supporters, in the composition of its institutions and in its activities. The Party Forum (*Forum des partis*) could outlaw any party that did not conform to the criteria of national unity. Nonetheless, it is difficult to ignore the fact that, from the outset, the most influential figure within the regime was Paul Kagame, the Tutsi commander of the RPF, who was appointed vice-president and minister of defence and, subsequently, president. Of the 22 ministers in the government, 9 came from the ranks of the RPF. Tutsi also constituted a majority in the new parliament, the army, and the security services.

In any event, Hutu-Tutsi harmony in the new government did not last long. In August 1995, the prime minister resigned because of his opposition to the government's policy toward the Hutu (non-implementation of the Arusha Accords, prohibiting the return of all Hutu refugees to Rwanda, and a policy of retribution). Five years later, in February 2000, the new prime minister, Pierre-Célestin Rwigema, resigned as well. One month later, in March 2000, President Bizimungu also resigned, voicing his objection to RPF policy that denied the existence of ethnic groups. He eventually formed his own distinctly Hutu party, the Democratic Party for Renewal (*Parti démocratique de renouveau*, or PDR). Bizimungu was imprisoned in 2001. Two years later, the MDR, Twagarimungu's party, was outlawed because it was accused of creating discord (*divisionisme*).

In 2003, a new constitution was approved by plebiscite by a huge majority of 93%. The constitution considerably strengthened the position of the president, who appoints the prime minister, the president of the supreme court, the regional governors, and the commanders of the security forces. Nevertheless, it also stated that the winning party could not appoint more than 50% of government ministers. That same year, elections were held for the presidency and for parliament. In the presidential elections, Kagame won 95% of the votes, and in the parliamentary elections the RPF, which he led, also won an overwhelming majority. The main opposition parties were Bizimungu's PDR, the *Alliance pour la démocratie, l'équité et le progrès* (ADEP-Mizero),[2] Twagarimungu's newly formed party, the *Parti démocrate centriste*, and the Peace Party (*Amahoro*), all of which were in essence (though not officially) Hutu parties. Additional opposition parties were the basically Tutsi monarchist parties—the *Union nationale rwandaise* (UNAR) and *Igihango*. There are grave doubts as to whether the elections were free and fair. Many argue that under RPF rule, the Rwandan authoritarian tradition, which we saw under the Tutsi monarchy in precolonial and colonial times and under Hutu republican rule in the years 1962–1994, continues.

Undoubtedly, Hutu-Tutsi tensions are still running high in the "new Rwanda." Although the RPF refers to a "mistake of ethnicity," many Tutsi regard the Hutu as "killers (Pottier 2002, 130, 131)." The Tutsi are convinced that only a Tutsi regime (even if not defined in such terms and not officially declared as such in public) can guarantee their security and survival. As a result, all sensitive positions related to defence, politics, and the media are held by Tutsi, who also regard themselves as responsible for the safety of their fellow Tutsi outside of Rwanda, primarily in Burundi and the Congo (DRC). There was particular concern regarding a possible power reversal in Burundi. Raids by Hutu rebels from the Democratic Republic of the Congo and from Burundi have also contributed to the continuation of Hutu-Tutsi tensions. In these crossborder raids, Tutsi were mur-

---

[2] "*Mizero*" means hope in Kinyarwanda.

dered for the sole reason that they were Tutsi—just like during the genocide. Furthermore, the fact that both Tutsi and Hutu witnesses who were about to testify against perpetrators were murdered does not indicate a harmonious relationship between the two groups. The Hutu also have their grievances: they complain that all key positions in state institutions are in Tutsi hands and that any criticism of Tutsi domination is suppressed because it is viewed as ethnic incitement. The Hutu are also angry that lands that were taken from Hutu who had fled to Congo (DRC) and given to Tutsi returning from Uganda were never returned to their original owners. Criticism by the Hutu is also directed at the government's compensation policy, which supports Tutsi families that were victims of the genocide, but refuse to support Hutu families whose family members had been murdered as moderate Hutus or as "traitors" to the Hutu cause. The government's refusal to put Tutsi RPF members on trial for "war crimes" also creates ill will and anger. The growing socioeconomic gap between the urban Tutsi population and the Hutu village population is another reason for Hutu bitterness.

In addition, the government also encounters heavy criticism from Tutsi hawks who oppose its "softness" toward the Hutu. They are particularly critical of the policy of amnesty for murderers and the support granted to Hutu refugees returning to Rwanda from the Congo (DRC). Again and again, complaints are heard about the fact that the support for Hutu refugees-returnees exceeds the support given to genocide survivors.

More than 15 years after the genocide (a concept the Hutu vehemently deny, since they choose to view it as it as a "civil war"), it is still quite impossible to write history books acceptable to both Hutu and Tutsi. This is a further indication that the government's "heroic" effort to be rid of the Hutu-Tutsi cleavage by denying its existence is nearly impossible to implement. There is also a built-in contradiction between the RPF position according to which there is only one people, not two different groups, and the ongoing talk about "genocide," which clearly presumes the existence of two ethnic groups (Pottier 2002, 126–131).

Cracks have also emerged in the new Tutsi establishment itself. There is considerable tension between English-speaking Tutsi from outside Rwanda, and French-speaking Tutsi who survived the genocide inside Rwanda. It is in this context that we must understand the January 2000 flight of Joseph Sebarenzi Kabuye, speaker of the Rwandan National Assembly, and the March 2000 murder of presidential advisor Assiel Kabera. Tensions also emerged between the republican Tutsi in power and the royalist Tutsi who wanted to restore the monarchy in the country.

At the same time, Hutu members of the "old" army (the FAR), the Presidential Guard, and the *Interahamwe*, all of whom were living in refugee camps in Zaire (which became the Democratic Republic of Congo in 1997), deployed new forces with the intention to invade Rwanda, defeat the RPF, and return the Hutu to power. FAR circles had ample financial resources for these activities, as they had left Rwanda with the country's treasury, and were supplied with weapons by various countries (including China) by way of Zaire. Until 1997, FAR activists benefited, among others, from the support of President Mobutu of Zaire, who assisted the Hutu government before and during the genocide and supported the Hutu militias in Burundi: the Forces for the Defence of Democracy (*Forces pour la défense de la démocratie*), or the FDD, and the National Forces of Liberation (*Forces nationales de libération*), or the FNL. President Habyarimana was actually buried in Mobutu's palace in Gbadolite.

The military activity of the old Rwandan regime ultimately resulted in tumultuous developments in Zaire/Congo/DRC as well. In conjunction with President Mobutu's forces, Hutu militias from Rwanda and Burundi began attacking and expelling the Tutsi in eastern Zaire/Congo (the *Banyamulenge*), who had been living there since the late nineteenth century. These developments led to an alliance between the Tutsi of Zaire/Congo/DRC and the guerilla forces of the *Alliance des Forces Démocratiques pour la libération du Congo-Zaïre* (AFDL), which was operating in the eastern Congo under the leadership of Laurent Desiré Kabila, and to the intervention of Rwandan and Ugandan forces on their behalf. As a result of the war, Kabila's (and Rwandan) forces entered Zaire's capital city of Kinshasa in May 1997, toppling Mobutu's regime and forcing him to flee to Morocco, where he died in 1998.

One year later, Congo was rocked by yet another major upheaval. As a result of the widespread hatred towards the Tutsi and the foreign armies of Rwanda and Uganda, President Kabila turned against his former allies. Again, an alliance was forged between Congo government forces and the forces of the old Hutu regime in Rwanda against rivals who were striving to topple his regime, and who were supported by the armies of Rwanda, Burundi, and Uganda. In the war fought in the Congo from 1998 onward, the armies of Angola and Zimbabwe intervened on behalf of President Kabila. Hundreds of thousands were killed in the bloody battles that ensued; some estimates place the total number of dead (including those who died of starvation or disease) at more than two million. In actuality, the war can be regarded as an extension of the civil wars in Rwanda and Burundi, since the fighting involved the Tutsi and Hutu armed forces of both countries (the official military and underground groups alike).

Another guerilla war emerged in northern Rwanda (primarily in the prefectures of Gisenyi and Ruhengeri) as a result of the invasion of Hutu guerilla forces of the Army for the Liberation of Rwanda (*Armée pour la libération du Rwanda* or ALR) from across the Congo border. The ALR is a group of rebels made up of the *Interahamwe* and the Rwandan armed forces who had been actively involved in the genocide in 1994. More than a decade after the genocide, estimates spoke of more than 50,000 Hutu soldiers and militiamen based in camps in the DRC and posing a mortal threat to the post-genocide government in Rwanda.

Solutions to the continuing hostilities and violence between the Hutu and the Tutsi have been discussed repeatedly. One suggestion is an "Israeli solution," which calls for the partitioning of Rwanda (and Burundi) into "Hutuland" and "Tutsiland." Such a partition, however, has been deemed unworkable because the two groups lack clearly defined territories. A second suggestion, a "Zanzibari solution,"[3] i.e. appending Rwanda to a larger country (such as Tanzania

---

3   Between 1830 and 1964, an Arab oligarchy ruled over a large African population in Zanzibar. In 1964, the country was subject to a violent revolution, in which many Arabs were killed. At that time, Zanzibar united with Tanganyika to form modern-day Tanzania. The rising tensions within Zanzibar, and between Zanzibar and the continental portion of Tanzania, were illustrative of the failure of this solution.

or the Congo) that could effectively engulf the local conflict, also seems impractical due to the chaos reigning in the Congo and the grave economic conditions prevailing in Tanzania. A third possibility, a "South African solution," involving the creation of a new non-ethnic Rwandan identity (similar to the "new" South African identity), is regarded as utopian in light of the genocide and the mutual massacres committed in Rwanda and Burundi, and which did not occur in South Africa (see Mamdani 2001, 264–265).

And so it seems that even after the "final solution," the people of the region may not enjoy peace and security. The threat of another genocide still hangs over the heads of the Tutsi, and perhaps the Hutu as well, not only in Rwanda, but also in Burundi and the Congo.

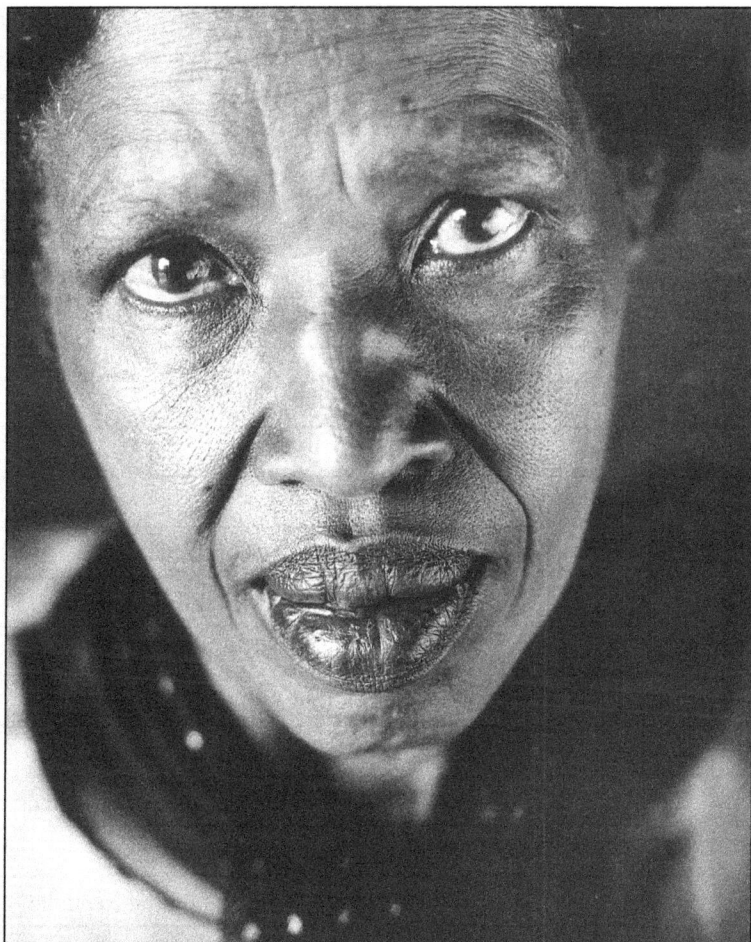

Illustration 12: "For the most part, I teach them [the students] that if the bad returns, they can say no"

I live practically alone. I sleep three hours a night. There are still people who can do me harm. Nonetheless, I am in a somewhat better state than I was. Some people find reasons to live. I am a teacher. I teach eight-year-old children. I don't talk to them about the genocide often. I tell them that it was something bad that surprised us. For the most part, I teach them that if the bad returns, they can say no. Some of these children have witnessed the most horrifying things, and when you speak with them you have to do so with great sensitivity. You have to tell them again and again that killing others is not a good thing, and that stealing and looting is bad.

Some understand this. There are others, orphans, who sit frustrated on their benches, with their heads in their hands. Maybe one day Hutus and Tutsis will be able to live together. (Marie Zisa, Age 62)

APPENDIX 1

THE HISTORY OF RWANDA: A CHRONOLOGY

Sixteenth century	Establishment of the historical Kingdom of Rwanda
1898	German conquest of Rwanda
1898–1916	German rule in Rwanda as part of German East Africa
1916	Belgian conquest of Rwanda
1916–1962	Belgian rule in Rwanda
1924	Belgian Mandate (League of Nations)
1933	Registration of ethnicity on Rwandan identity cards
1957	Publication of the "Hutu Manifesto"
November 1, 1959	Onset of the "Hutu Revolution"
1960	PARMEHUTU victory in local elections
1961	PARMEHUTU victory in parliamentary elections
July 1, 1962	Independence
1962	Kayibanda elected president of the First Republic
1962–1964	Tens of thousands of Tutsi murdered, hundreds of thousands of Tutsis become refugees, invasion of Tutsi guerilla forces
July 1, 1973	Military coup by General Habyarimana
1973–1994	Second Republic under President Habyarimana
1978	Establishment of single-party dictatorship
1987	RPF established in Uganda
October 1, 1990	RPF invades Rwanda
October 4, 1990	France and Belgium send troops to Rwanda
October 1990	Anti-Tutsi mass violence
January–March 1991	Anti-Tutsi mass violence

July 1991	Rwandan authorities consent to the establishment of opposition parties
August 1991	"Bloc" of opposition parties established
March, August 1991	Anti-Tutsi mass violence
April 1992	Opposition parties join government coalition
July 12, 1992	First ceasefire agreement between Rwandan government forces and the RPF
January–February 1992	Anti-Tutsi mass violence
February 1992	RPF offensive on northern Rwanda, mass flight of Hutu inhabitants
March 7, 1992	Second ceasefire agreement signed in Dar es Salam
July 1993	RTLMC radio station goes on the air
August 4, 1993	Arusha Accords
October 5, 1993	UN Security Council resolution establishing UNAMIR
October 23, 1993	"Hutu Power" campaign launched
November 1993	UN forces arrive in Rwanda
December 28, 1993	RPF ministers and RPA battalion arrive in Kigali
April 5, 1994	UN Security Council extends the mandate of the UN force in Rwanda
April 6, 1994	Assassination of President Habyarimana by surface-to-air missile
April 6–11, 1994	Rwandan genocide—Phase I: selective killings of Tutsi elite and moderate Hutu
April 9–14, 1994	Belgian-French evacuation force operates in country
April 11–July 15, 1994	Rwandan genocide—Phase II: final solution, 800,000 Tutsi killed
April 21, 1994	Security Council resolution to withdraw the bulk of the UN force from Rwanda
May 17, 1994	Security Council resolution calls for an end to the violence and mass killing, for an embargo on the provision of arms to Rwanda and establishes UNAMIR II
May 26, 1994	US embargo on the provision of arms to Rwanda

June 22, 1994	UN authorizes Member States to set up a multinational operation for humanitarian purposes, which will: "Contribute to the security and protection of displaced persons, refugees and civilians at risk in Rwanda, including through the establishment and maintenance, where feasible, of secure humanitarian areas."
June 28, 1994	First reference to the events in Rwanda as "genocidal acts" by the UN Commission on Human Rights
July 5, 1994	RPF occupation of Kigali
July 15, 1994	RPF forces establish control over all of Rwanda (except for the Secure Humanitarian Zone established by the French)
July 18, 1994	RPF forms new Rwandan government
August 21, 1994	Completion of withdrawal of French forces
1996–1997	War in the Congo (involving the new Rwandan army) to topple President Mobutu
1998–2003	War in the Congo (involving the old and new Rwandan army and the Hutu militias)

APPENDIX 2

THE GENOCIDE AS DESCRIBED BY RWANDAN AUTHORS

Don't Be Afraid to Know
(Mukagasana 1999, 189–191, 247–248)

Yolande Mukagasana, a Rwandan Tutsi genocide survivor, is the author of three books: two depicting her own experiences during and following the killings, and a third that includes interviews with and photographs of both survivors and perpetrators of the genocide. In the course of the 1994 genocide, Mukagasana lost her husband Joseph and her three children, Christian, Sandrine, and Nadine, as well as numerous friends and acquaintances. Her only surviving sibling was her older brother Kalisa, who was married to a Hutu woman whom he loved deeply, but who abandoned him, cutting off all contact with him. In her book *N'aie pas peur de savoir* (*Don't be Afraid to Know*), Mukagasana recounts her first encounter after the killings with Kalisa and with her niece Spérancie, who had tried to save Yolande's children. Both stories are presented below.

In January, my brother was severely beaten by the *Interahamwe* in the city of Butare, where he lived. It was three days before we found him in a ditch, unconscious and almost completely paralyzed. I took him from hospital to hospital in Butare. No doctor could treat him. In despair, I finally brought him to the Chinese hospital in Kibungo in eastern Rwanda where he received acupuncture treatments. He remained there for three months. One week before the assassination of [President] Habyarimana, I gave him some money, as I felt that the murders were just around the corner.

You know, Kalisa, when the genocide began, I was convinced they had killed you in Kibungo.

In the hospital, they killed the people in their beds. But I fled on my crutches like a crazy man, through the fields, into a bushy thicket. There were times that I found cars to take me a few dozen kilometers further. I did what all Tutsi did. I got rid of my identity card. I wanted to reach Butare, because I had heard that killings were not happening there. But when I reached Gitarama, I could not walk any more. Eventually, I was hospitalized by the Red Cross in Kabgayi, where I found myself in a room next to your neighbor Noël Hitimana, the RTLM correspondent whose death was announced on the morning of April 7. By chance, he did not recognize me.

You know, I wanted to tell him that I was your brother and to ask him if it was true that you had been killed. But I couldn't do it. The hospital was full of FAR [Rwandan army] soldiers and extremists. As you can imagine, my life was not worth very much. They came to check on me every day, not in order to treat me but because they suspected that I was a Tutsi. "What's that?" they said. "That guy's definitely a Tutsi. Look at his nose and his small crafty eyes."

"I once saw him bathing," said another proudly. He has stretch marks like Tutsi women."

I spent every moment awaiting my death. One day, a nurse came into my room and told me quietly: "Listen, I know that they're coming to kill you. Be strong and remain brave. Accept it like everyone else. I will pray for you." I stayed in bed and pondered death. It seemed inevitable.

But didn't you try to run?

Run? That's impossible. Soldiers were guarding all the exits. Suddenly, some soldiers entered the room. "Let's go, everybody up. Everyone's leaving. The FPR is closing in and we need to flee."

My brother broke into laughter, but I could sense the sorrow in his laugh.

Everyone got up except me. I hid under the sheet, and then I slipped quietly under the bed. They loaded the wounded on busses as morning approached. I stayed under my bed for two hours, and then I heard footsteps in the hall. A despondent looking Hutu boy who had been hospitalized with malaria appeared in the doorway. Here he is. Say hello.

The boy greeted me almost ceremonially.

"What's your name?"

"Kabera."

"Where's your family?"

"They all fled to Zaire."

"Why didn't they take you with them?"

"They abandoned me."

"Why?"

"Because I didn't know when they left." Kalisa continued his story.

Kabera told me that the hospital was completely deserted. Deserted? And what is that shooting? "The shooting is the government army fighting the FPR, a bit farther away." Then I got up on my crutches and sat with the boy in the doorway.

Why didn't you stay in hiding?

Stay in hiding? I couldn't take it anymore. All I wanted was to die.

Die? Just when it looked like you had a chance to live?

I don't know, Yolande. That's how it is. You know, I should have never married Zéphanie. Her family never accepted me, because I am a Tutsi. The genocide was stronger than our love. I wanted to die. I waited for soldiers from the FAR or the *Interahamwe* to come and cut off my head. But then a soldier came and started to interrogate me. "Hey old man! How are things?—Alright.—Where are the others?—I don't know.—Where did they go?—I don't know.—And why did you stay behind?—I don't know. They didn't take me. It was almost only soldiers here.—What about you? Aren't you a soldier?—No.—What's your story."

I told him everything. I don't know if he believed me, but they sent me to a hospital in Nyanza, and then to Bugesera. The Red Cross treated me there.

Yolande Mukagasana, a nurse by profession, ran a health clinic that treated poor people in the neighborhood for free; she was known as muganga (doctor). She was well thought of in the surrounding area and therefore particularly hunted down by the murderers. Her husband Joseph sacrificed himself to save her and their children. He reported to one of the thousands of checkpoints in Rwanda where everyone's identity card was checked. Every card contained information about the cardholder's "ethnicity." Tutsi were typically killed on the spot. By the time the *Interahamwe* finished dealing with Joseph, Yolande and the children had managed to escape. Since she had been specially marked as a target for assassination, Yolande thought the children would be safer with one of her nieces, a Hutu whom she calls Spérancie in her books. However, the killers came to her niece's apartment, beat everyone there, forced them to undress completely, and marched them to a pre-dug ditch to which other Tutsi had also been taken. There, they were all hacked to death with machetes and thrown into the ditch. After one of the murderers identified Spérancie as a Hutu, they simply ignored her, even though she ran from one murderer to the next and begged them to kill her as well. After the genocide, Spérancie met Yolande and told her about the death of her children. She did not, however, tell her what happened to her next. This she shared with her only a short time before Yolande travelled to Belgium. And even then she did not tell her everything. Here is the conversation between them.

The day they killed your children, as you might remember, they stripped and banished me. I walked naked along the path like a crazy woman, with my clothes in a pile on my head. I went home, but the house was already destroyed and looted. So I got dressed and went to Cécile's house.

Cécile? Côme's wife?

Yes.

What were you thinking?! Côme is one of the worst murderers of all. He kicked me out of his house right in the middle of the genocide.

Listen. First of all, my house was destroyed. So was yours. All our Tutsi neighbors had been killed and all their homes were in ruins. Where should I have gone? I also had no idea that he was a mass murderer. After all, he was a friend of yours before the genocide. I stood before him, and Cécile looked at me in shock. Still, I was suspicious. I told her that you had been killed along with your children, and she looked pleased. I asked if I could stay with her for a few days, and she agreed. Just then, the *Interahamwe* showed up. I picked up a broom and started sweeping the yard, as if I were one of her employees. But Cécile took the broom from me and announced loudly that she did not know me.

The *Interahamwe* surrounded me and demanded to see my identity card. "I don't have it!" I cried. "I'm Hutu, I swear!" One of the *Interahamwe* confirmed it, but the tension continued to rise.

"Where is your sister [aunt] Muganga? Tell us or we'll kill you." I was trembling. I swore I was not your sister, and the *Interahamwe* again confirmed. "I don't care!" bellowed one *Interahamwe* man. "Tell us where Muganga is!"

"I don't know. I swear."

I was less than one hundred meters away, hiding under a sink.

I broke into nervous, almost wicked laughter.

You were one hundred meters away?

Yes, yes, Spérancie, under Emmanuelle's sink!

Heavens! If I had only known! I would have come to hide with you. But I'll continue. Apparently, the *Interahamwe* were disappointed with my answer. "Where is Muganga?" They screamed, "Where is Muganga?" I continued telling them that I did not know where you were hiding. And then, calmly, one of them slapped me. "Open your mouth!" he ordered. I opened my mouth. "Wider," he said. I tried.

"Wider!" And then suddenly, he pulled a grenade from his belt and shoved it in my mouth. My mouth was too small, so he punched it and the grenade went in, and broke this tooth. I went out of my mind. I started running in all different directions among the *Interahamwe* men, who just stood there laughing. I tried to pull out the grenade, but I wasn't able to. It was stuck in my mouth like a piece of fruit that was too big. I ran around like a madwoman as my life flashed quickly before my eyes. Again, I saw your children falling into the ditch.

Spérancie's gaze fixed on a piece of paper on the ground. She remained quiet for a long time, and I was unable to find a sentence or even a word to say to her. At that point, we were both undoubtedly thinking about death. Then Spérancie resumed talking, in a more serious tone.

I don't know how long it lasted. It was about fifteen minutes later when I realized that the grenade had not exploded, and that all the *Interahamwe* men were gone. I again found myself on the path. Now a different man approached me. I stood there, unable to speak, with the grenade that I had not managed to extricate. The man helped me, he got the grenade out of my mouth, and we saw that they had not removed the pin. Aunt, that's something that I kept secret for months, and I couldn't talk about it. You know, I was so certain that I was dead that I was no longer able to speak. I felt dead inside.

Murambi, the Book of Bones
(Diop 2006, 17–19, 87–89, 97–99)

Boubacar Boris Diop is a renowned Senegalese novelist. He writes in French and Wolof, his native language, and is well informed about events across the African continent. However, like many other Africans, he knew very little about Rwanda. When the mass extermination occurred, he initially reacted wearily, as if this was simply another case of "blacks killing blacks," consistent with all the racist stereotypes. "I spoke about Rwanda," he explained later, "without knowing anything about the country, unaware that I needed to learn about it. I was drawn into a mystification of sorts shared by many today— even Africans—according to which the same forces are at work and the same violence at play in Liberia, Sierra Leone, and Somalia. That's how I fulfilled my obligation. I contributed my small quota of tears, and moved on." He only discovered the Rwandan genocide in 1998, during the few months he spent in Rwanda with a group of African and Western authors and intellectuals as part of a project of the African literature and arts festival, "Africa Fest." Since his visit to Rwanda, he says, his "life and thinking revolve around the extermination."

As a result of the visit, he wrote Murambi, *Le livre des ossements* (Murambi, the Book of Bones). In addition to its main plot, the book contains chapters—some of which are extremely short— written in the first person by perpetrators, survivors, and witnesses. What follows are three chapters, each of which can be read on its own. According to Diop, he listened for hours to her story.

Rosa Karemera
(Diop 2006, 97–99)

Yesterday morning I thought my time had come. At my age I couldn't run like the others. In addition, there was this awful barricade a few yards from my house. For several days now, the *Interahamwe* have been performing all their dirty business there. I knew that Valérie Rumiya, a Hutu woman who lives at the other end of our street, had almost gone crazy from the beginning of this mess. She's always hated me—because, she claims, I always look down on everyone, I never say hello, I act like a grand lady, etc. She went from barricade to barricade to ask the *Interahamwe*: "And that Rosa Karemera, are you quite sure you've killed her?" Finally, she was bothering everyone, and so to get rid of her, the *Interahamwe* answered, "Of course Mama, that's been taken care of." Then she tried to catch them out: "Tell me what Rosa Karemera looks like, and I'll know if you're telling me the truth! Come on, tell me you little liars!" The *Interahamwe*, caught off guard at first, didn't know what to reply, then they burst out laughing. Quite a case, this Granny Valérie. They tried to reassure her: "But Mama, there's no way of knowing, we've killed so many people! No Inyenzi from this neighborhood has had the time to run away." In spite of that, she didn't trust them and continued to ask the same question all over the place.

Her idea of a genocide, that bitch, is just that: to get me, Rosa Karemera, killed. I can't even stick my nose out. So the day before yesterday, through a superhuman effort, I jumped over the wall and landed in the house of my Hutu neighbors. The father, panic-stricken at first, told me that he didn't want to have any problems with the government, then he allowed me to stay. A good man, really, who listened to his heart. But that pest of a Valérie Rumiya found out and gave me away.

Then a soldier from the presidential guard—a warrant officer, I think—arrived. He was really angry. He said, "Here in Butare, you're creating too many problems. You think you're smarter than everyone else just because you have a university degree. You hide Inyenzi. If you don't turn in the woman who's in this house, I'll spray you all!" He drew a sort of semi-circle with his rifle. Ah! These young people are having a fine time these days. We were lined up in the courtyard. I got out of line, I walked up to him dragging my leg—I've limped since birth, polio—and I said, "Here I am, I'm the woman you're looking for." I wasn't scared anymore. I wanted then to get it over and done with. He turned toward me, looked at me from head to toe, and immediately I saw how disappointed he was. Valérie Rumiya must have told him that I was one of the spies that the RPF had been infiltrating in the main cities for the past five weeks. He had imagined me to be arrogant, very tall, beautiful, and, in a nutshell, disturbingly sensual, and there I was, just a poor scrap of an old woman, crippled besides. The Hutu family who had hidden me were there and everyone looked at him silently. You could easily see his embarrassment. They he declared brusquely, turning the barrel of his gun down toward the ground: "OK. Give me ten thousand francs for the kids' beer." They gave him the money and he left. Of course I had to change hiding place and I hope to survive this business. Just to see the look on Valérie Rumiya's face when she runs in to me in the neighborhood.

Marina Nkusi
(Diop 2006, 87–89)

We called him Tonton Antoine. For as far back as I can remember, I always saw him at the house. He was my father's best friend. Actually, his only friend, I think. Already, when I was a little girl, I had the feeling that he wasn't like anyone else we knew. He didn't laugh very much, but he loved doing magic tricks with cards. Projecting the shadows of his fingers against a wall, he could also create tortoises or dragonflies. As soon as I saw him arrive I would rush out to meet him. He would lift me up on his shoulders and run around our place singing, "Marina has an airplane, Tonton Antoine is little Marina's airplane!" I was, I think, one of the few people who could cheer him up.

A few days after the events, he came to the house a first time. He and my father talked for a long time in low voices.

We knew that he was in charge of several barricades in Kibuye. Nonetheless, he had a sweet face, if a little bit sad, just as I'd known him from my earliest childhood.

When he left, my father seemed to be very preoccupied.

"Does he know that we're hiding those little ones here?" asked my mother, worried.

"No, but he says I should take up my machete like all the other men."

"Ah?"

"I refused. I can't do that."

My mother said nothing. After a while he cried out again:

"Yes, I refused!"

Two days passed.

Tonton Antoine came back.

He and my father locked themselves away again in the living room. For the first time in my life I heard Tonton Antoine shout.

After this second meeting my father started to change. He talked to himself, wandering from one room to another: "Ah! I can't agree to do it, those people have never done anything to me! It's savagery!"

The next instant he would say that he had to protect us. If he didn't do anything, the *Interahamwe* were going to come and kill everyone in the house. The third day, not being able to stand it anymore, he took up his machete. My mother and I wanted to keep him from going out. Then he screamed, "Don't you watch the television? It's like all wars, you kill people and then its over!"

He went to the barricade. They tell us that he handles his machete like a maniac over there.

However, when he's back at the house, he goes straight to the little ones' hiding place, he gives them treats and plays with them. Then he retires to his bedroom. Mother and I don't dare disturb him.

When he leaves very early the next morning, we pretend we're still asleep.

Faustin Gasana
(Diop 2006, 17–19)

Faustin Gasana, a young boss in *Interahamwe*, was surrounded by his family and friends on the eve of the exterminations in the prefecture of Kibango—his sisters, who prepared the mint tea he liked, and his neighbors, who expressed their support for the impending "work" as the killings were referred to. Faustin's father, bedridden and extremely ill, summoned his son to his room. "The old man," an almost historic figure, had always harbored racist feelings toward the Tutsi. In contrast to everyone else, however, he was despondent and enraged as he was convinced that none of the men set to undertake the "work" was up to the task: he feared that they would be distracted and weakened by beer, rape, greed, and simple exhaustion. An ideological pedagogue, he repeated what he had already told Faustin dozens of times. Below is an excerpt of their conversation.

"Surely you've heard of the Frenchman who wanted to kill all the white Inyenzi during their big war there…"

"He was a German."

"What was his name?"

I feel a bit annoyed. I've never liked his odd habit of asking questions that, in many cases, he often already knows the answers to.

"Hitler."

"Hitler what?" he insists, studying me with his malicious eyes.

"Adolf. Adolph Hitler. They called him the Führer," I added, in order to preempt the next question.

"So tell me: Did he succeed in eliminating all the white Inyenzi?"

I refuse to go there. I've had enough of this drivel. All this time wasted …

I say, "We'll talk about it again some other time. I have to go."

Very angry, he shouts:

"That white man was much better organized than you but he failed. You're nothing but a pretentious little bunch of idiots!"

I get up. "Work's waiting for me," I say, trying to appear calm.

"You're mad, aren't you? How dare you get mad at your father?"

"Don't be angry. I have to go because we are starting tonight here in Kibango."

He replies calmly.

"Go away. You're a generation of incompetents."

He has lowered his voice to put into it all the force he can muster, which makes his words sound even more terrible.

I'm fond of the old man. He's my father. But he's like all those old people who discover miraculous answers to the world's problems on their deathbed. Things aren't so simple. I've always known in becoming an *Interahamwe* that I might well have to kill people myself or perish under their blows. That's never been a problem for me. I've studied the history of my country and I know that the Tutsis and us, we could never live together. Never. Lot's of shirkers claim otherwise, but I don't believe it. I'm going to do my work properly. And I agree with the old man: every time you hurl insults at someone who's about to die, you give someone else the time to escape. I'm not so stupid that I can't see that. But how do I get that into my men's heads?

APPENDIX 3

STATUTE OF THE INTERNATIONAL CRIMINAL TRIBUNAL FOR RWANDA AS ADOPTED AND AMENDED, AS APPLICABLE, BY THE FOLLOWING SECURITY COUNCIL RESOLUTIONS

1.	Resolution 955 (1994) 8 November 1994	Establishing the International Criminal Tribunal for Rwanda (ICTR) and attaches its Statute.
2.	Resolution 1165 (1998) 30 April 1998	Establishing a third Trial Chamber and amends Articles 10, 11 and 12 of the ICTR Statute.
3.	Resolution 1329 (2000) 30 November 2000	Deciding that two additional elected ICTR judges will sit in the Appeals Chamber.
4.	Resolution 1411 (2002) 17 May 2002	Amending Article 11 of the ICTR Statute on composition of the Chambers.
5.	Resolution 1431 (2002) 14 August 2002	Establishing a pool of 18 ICTR *ad litem* judges and amending Articles 11, 12 and 13 of the ICTR Statute.
6.	Resolution 1503 (2003) 28 August 2003	Urging the ICTR to formalize a completion strategy, amending Article 15 of the Statute on "The Prosecutor," and calling on the International Criminal Tribunal for the former Yugoslavia (ICTY) and the ICTR to complete investigations by the end of 2004, all trials at first instance by the end of 2008, and all work in 2010.

7.	Resolution 1512 (2003) 27 October 2003	Increasing the number of *ad litem* judges who may be appointed at any one time to serve in a trial chamber and amending Articles 11 and 12 *quater* of the Statute.
8.	Resolution 1534 (2004) 26 March 2004	Calling on the ICTY and ICTR Prosecutors to identify cases that should be transferred to national jurisdictions and requesting the Tribunals to provide assessments of the implementation of their respective completion strategies every 6 months.
9.	Resolution 1684 (2006) 13 June 2006	Extending the term of office of the 11 permanent ICTR Judges through 31 December 2008.
10.	Resolution 1717 (2006) 13 October 2006	Extending through 31 December 2008 the term of office of the ICTR *ad litem* Judges elected in June 2003.
11.	Resolution 1824 (2008) 18 July 2008	Extending through 31 December 2009 the term of office of the ICTR Trial Judges (*ad litem* and permanent), and through 31 December 2010 the term of office of the two ICTR Appeals Judges, and amending Article 11 of the ICTR Statute.
12.	Resolution 1855 (2008) 19 December 2008	Amending Article 11 of the ICTR Statute and therefore extending the number of *ad litem* Judges allowed at the Tribunal.
13.	Resolution 1878 (2009) 7 July 2009	Amending Article 13 of the ICTR Statute and therefore increasing the composition of the Appeals Chamber.

14.	Resolution 1901 (2009) 16 December 2009	Underlining its intention to extend, by 30 June 2010, the terms of office of all trial and appeals judges; temporarily increasing the number of *ad litem* judges allowed at the Tribunal at any one time; deciding that one ICTR trial judge complete his case, notwithstanding the expiry of his term of office.

As amended by the Security Council acting under Chapter VII of the Charter of the United Nations, the International Criminal Tribunal for the Prosecution of Persons Responsible for Genocide and Other Serious Violations of International Humanitarian Law Committed in the Territory of Rwanda and Rwandan Citizens responsible for genocide and other such violations committed in the territory of neighboring States, between 1 January 1994 and 31 December 1994 (hereinafter referred to as "The International Tribunal for Rwanda") shall function in accordance with the provisions of the present Statute.

Article 1
Competence of the International Tribunal for Rwanda

The International Tribunal for Rwanda shall have the power to prosecute persons responsible for serious violations of international humanitarian law committed in the territory of Rwanda and Rwandan citizens responsible for such violations committed in the territory of neighbouring States between 1 January 1994 and 31 December 1994, in accordance with the provisions of the present Statute.

Article 2
Genocide

1. The International Tribunal for Rwanda shall have the power to prosecute persons committing genocide as defined in paragraph 2 of this Article or of committing any of the other acts enumerated in paragraph 3 of this Article.

2. Genocide means any of the following acts committed with intent to destroy, in whole or in part, a national, ethnical, racial or religious group, as such:

(a) Killing members of the group;

(b) Causing serious bodily or mental harm to members of the group;

(c) Deliberately inflicting on the group conditions of life calculated to bring about its physical destruction in whole or in part;

(d) Imposing measures intended to prevent births within the group;

(e) Forcibly transferring children of the group to another group.

3. The following acts shall be punishable:

(a) Genocide;

(b) Conspiracy to commit genocide;

(c) Direct and public incitement to commit genocide;

(d) Attempt to commit genocide;

(e) Complicity in genocide.

Article 3
Crimes against Humanity

The International Tribunal for Rwanda shall have the power to prosecute persons responsible for the following crimes when committed as part of a widespread or systematic attack against any civilian population on national, political, ethnic, racial or religious grounds:

(a) Murder;

(b) Extermination;

(c) Enslavement;

(d) Deportation;

(e) Imprisonment;

(f) Torture;

(g) Rape;

(h) Persecutions on political, racial and religious grounds;

(i) Other inhumane acts.

Article 4

Violations of Article 3 Common to the Geneva Conventions and of Additional Protocol II

The International Tribunal for Rwanda shall have the power to prosecute persons committing or ordering to be committed serious violations of Article 3 common to the Geneva Conventions of 12 August 1949 for the Protection of War Victims, and of Additional Protocol II thereto of 8 June 1977. These violations shall include, but shall not be limited to:

(a) Violence to life, health and physical or mental well-being of persons, in particular murder as well as cruel treatment such as torture, mutilation or any form of corporal punishment;

(b) Collective punishments;

(c) Taking of hostages;

(d) Acts of terrorism;

(e) Outrages upon personal dignity, in particular humiliating and degrading treatment, rape, enforced prostitution and any form of indecent assault;

(f) Pillage;

(g) The passing of sentences and the carrying out of executions without previous judgment pronounced by a regularly constituted court, affording all the judicial guarantees which are recognized as indispensable by civilized peoples;

(h) Threats to commit any of the foregoing acts.

Article 5
Personal Jurisdiction

The International Tribunal for Rwanda shall have jurisdiction over natural persons pursuant to the provisions of the present Statute.

Article 6
Individual Criminal Responsibility

1. A person who planned, instigated, ordered, committed or otherwise aided and abetted in the planning, preparation or execution of a crime referred to in Articles 2 to 4 of the present Statute, shall be individually responsible for the crime.

2. The official position of any accused person, whether as head of state or government or as a responsible government official, shall not relieve such person of criminal responsibility nor mitigate punishment.

3. The fact that any of the acts referred to in Articles 2 to 4 of the present Statute was committed by a subordinate does not relieve his or her superior of criminal responsibility if he or she knew or had reason to know that the subordinate was about to commit such acts or had done so and the superior failed to take the necessary and reasonable measures to prevent such acts or to punish the perpetrators thereof.

4. The fact that an accused person acted pursuant to an order of a government or of a superior shall not relieve him or her of criminal responsibility, but may be considered in mitigation of punishment if the International Tribunal for Rwanda determines that justice so requires.

Article 7
Territorial and Temporal Jurisdiction

The territorial jurisdiction of the International Tribunal for Rwanda shall extend to the territory of Rwanda including its land surface and airspace as well as to the territory of neighboring States in respect of serious violations of international humanitarian law committed by Rwandan citizens. The temporal jurisdiction of the International Tribunal for Rwanda shall extend to a period beginning on 1 January 1994 and ending on 31 December 1994.

Article 8
Concurrent Jurisdiction

1. The International Tribunal for Rwanda and national courts shall have concurrent jurisdiction to prosecute persons for serious violations of international humanitarian law committed in the territory of Rwanda and Rwandan citizens for such violations committed in the territory of the neighboring States, between 1 January 1994 and 31 December 1994.

2. The International Tribunal for Rwanda shall have the primacy over the national courts of all States. At any stage of the procedure, the International Tribunal for Rwanda may formally request national courts to defer to its competence in accordance with the present Statute and the Rules of Procedure and Evidence of the International Tribunal for Rwanda.

Article 9
Non bis in idem[1]

1. No person shall be tried before a national court for acts constituting serious violations of international humanitarian law under the present Statute, for which he or she has already been tried by the International Tribunal for Rwanda.
2. A person who has been tried before a national court for acts constituting serious violations of international humanitarian law may be subsequently tried by the International Tribunal for Rwanda only if:
(a) The act for which he or she was tried was characterized as an ordinary crime; or
(b) The national court proceedings were not impartial or independent, were designed to shield the accused from international criminal responsibility, or the case was not diligently prosecuted.

---

[1] A Latin phrase signifying double jeopardy, i.e. no person shall be tried twice for the same crime.

3. In considering the penalty to be imposed on a person convicted of a crime under the present Statute, the International Tribunal for Rwanda shall take into account the extent to which any penalty imposed by a national court on the same person for the same act has already been served.

Article 10

Organization of the International Tribunal for Rwanda

The International Tribunal for Rwanda shall consist of the following organs:

(a) The Chambers, comprising three Trial Chambers and an Appeals Chamber;

(b) The Prosecutor;

(c) A Registry.

Article 11

Composition of the Chambers

1. The Chambers shall be composed of a maximum of sixteen permanent independent judges, no two of whom may be nationals of the same State, and a maximum at any one time of nine *ad litem* independent judges appointed in accordance with article 12 *ter*, paragraph 2, of the present Statute, no two of whom may be nationals of the same State.

2. Each Trial Chamber may be divided into sections of three judges each, composed of both permanent and *ad litem* judges. A section of a Trial Chamber shall have the same powers and responsibilities as a Trial Chamber under the present Statute and shall render judgment in accordance with the same rules.

3. Seven of the permanent judges shall be members of the Appeals Chamber. The Appeals Chamber shall, for each appeal, be composed of five of its members.

4. A person who for the purposes of membership of the Chambers of the International Tribunal for Rwanda could be regarded as a national of more than one State shall be deemed to be a national of the State in which that person ordinarily exercises civil and political rights.

Article 12
Qualification and Election of Judges

The permanent and *ad litem* judges shall be persons of high moral character, impartiality and integrity who possess the qualifications required in their respective countries for appointment to the highest judicial offices. In the overall composition of the Chambers and sections of the Trial Chambers, due account shall be taken of the experience of the judges in criminal law, international law, including international humanitarian law and human rights law.

Article 12
bis: Election of Permanent Judges

1. Eleven of the permanent judges of the International Tribunal for Rwanda shall be elected by the General Assembly from a list submitted by the Security Council, in the following manner:

(a) The Secretary-General shall invite nominations for permanent judges of the International Tribunal for Rwanda from States Members of the United Nations and non-member States maintaining permanent observer missions at United Nations Headquarters;

(b) Within sixty days of the date of the invitation of the Secretary-General, each State may nominate up to two candidates meeting the qualifications set out in article 12 of the present Statute, no two of whom shall be of the same nationality and neither of whom shall be of the same nationality as any judge who is a member of the Appeals Chamber and who was elected or appointed a permanent judge of the International Tribunal for the Prosecution of Persons Responsible for Serious Violations of International Humanitarian Law Committed in the Territory of the Former Yugoslavia since 1991 (hereinafter referred to as 'the International Tribunal for the Former Yugoslavia') in accordance with article 13 *bis* of the Statute of that Tribunal;

(c) The Secretary-General shall forward the nominations received to the Security Council. From the nominations received the Security Council shall establish a list of not less than twenty-two and not more than thirty-three candidates, taking due account of the adequate representation on the International Tribunal for Rwanda of the principal legal systems of the world;

(d) The President of the Security Council shall transmit the list of candidates to the President of the General Assembly. From that list the General Assembly shall elect eleven permanent judges of the International Tribunal for Rwanda. The candidates who receive an absolute majority of the votes of the States Members of the United Nations and of the non-member States maintaining permanent observer missions at United Nations Headquarters, shall be declared elected. Should two candidates of the same nationality obtain the required majority vote, the one who received the higher number of votes shall be considered elected.

2. In the event of a vacancy in the Chambers amongst the permanent judges elected or appointed in accordance with this article, after consultation with the Presidents of the Security Council and of the General Assembly, the Secretary-General shall appoint a person meeting the qualifications of article 12 of the present Statute, for the remainder of the term of office concerned.

3. The permanent judges elected in accordance with this article shall be elected for a term of four years. The terms and conditions of service shall be those of the permanent judges of the International Tribunal for the Former Yugoslavia. They shall be eligible for re-election.

Article 12
ter: Election and Appointment of *ad litem* Judges[2]

1. The *ad litem* judges of the International Tribunal for Rwanda shall be elected by the General Assembly from a list submitted by the Security Council, in the following manner:

(a) The Secretary-General shall invite nominations for *ad litem* judges of the International Tribunal for Rwanda from States Members of the United Nations and non-member States maintaining permanent observer missions at United Nations Headquarters;

(b) Within sixty days of the date of the invitation of the Secretary-General, each State may nominate up to four candidates meeting the qualifications

---

[2]   *ad litem*, i.e. acting in a lawsuit on behalf of a child or person who is not considered capable of representing him or herself.

set out in article 12 of the present Statute, taking into account the importance of a fair representation of female and male candidates;

(c) The Secretary-General shall forward the nominations received to the Security Council. From the nominations received the Security Council shall establish a list of not less than thirty-six candidates, taking due account of the adequate representation of the principal legal systems of the world and bearing in mind the importance of equitable geographical distribution;

(d) The President of the Security Council shall transmit the list of candidates to the President of the General Assembly. From that list the General Assembly shall elect the eighteen *ad litem* judges of the International Tribunal for Rwanda. The candidates who receive an absolute majority of the votes of the States Members of the United Nations and of the non-member States maintaining permanent observer missions at United Nations Headquarters shall be declared elected;

(e) The *ad litem* judges shall be elected for a term of four years. They shall not be eligible for re-election.

2. During their term, *ad litem* judges will be appointed by the Secretary-General, upon request of the President of the International Tribunal for Rwanda, to serve in the Trial Chambers for one or more trials, for a cumulative period of up to, but not including, three years. When requesting the appointment of any particular *ad litem* judge, the President of the International Tribunal for Rwanda shall bear in mind the criteria set out in article 12 of the present Statute regarding the composition of the Chambers and sections of the Trial Chambers, the considerations set out in paragraphs 1 (b) and (c) above and the number of votes the *ad litem* judge received in the General Assembly.

Article 12
quater: Status of *ad litem* Judges

1. During the period in which they are appointed to serve in the International Tribunal for Rwanda, *ad litem* judges shall:

(a) Benefit from the same terms and conditions of service mutatis mutandis as the permanent judges of the International Tribunal for Rwanda;

(b) Enjoy, subject to paragraph 2 below, the same powers as the permanent judges of the International Tribunal for Rwanda;

(c) Enjoy the privileges and immunities, exemptions and facilities of a judge of the International Tribunal for Rwanda;

(d) Enjoy the power to adjudicate in pre-trial proceedings in cases other than those that they have been appointed to try.

2. During the period in which they are appointed to serve in the International Tribunal for Rwanda, *ad litem* judges shall not:

(a) Be eligible for election as, or to vote in the election of, the President of the International Tribunal for Rwanda or the Presiding Judge of a Trial Chamber pursuant to article 13 of the present Statute;

(b) Have power:

(i) To adopt rules of procedure and evidence pursuant to article 14 of the present Statute. They shall, however, be consulted before the adoption of those rules;

(ii) To review an indictment pursuant to article 18 of the present Statute;

(iii) To consult with the President of the International Tribunal for Rwanda in relation to the assignment of judges pursuant to article 13 of the present Statute or in relation to a pardon or commutation of sentence pursuant to article 27 of the present Statute.

Article 13
Officers and Members of the Chambers

1. The permanent judges of the International Tribunal for Rwanda shall elect a President from amongst their number.

2. The President of the International Tribunal for Rwanda shall be a member of one of its Trial Chambers.

3. After consultation with the permanent judges of the International Tribunal for Rwanda, the President shall assign two of the permanent judges elected or appointed in accordance with article 12 *bis* of the present Statute to be members of the Appeals Chamber of the International Tribunal for the Former Yugoslavia and eight to the Trial Chambers of the International Tribunal for Rwanda. Notwithstanding the provisions of article 11, paragraph 1, and article

11, paragraph 3, the President may assign to the Appeals Chamber up to four additional permanent judges serving in the Trial Chambers, on the completion of the cases to which each judge is assigned. The term of office of each judge redeployed to the Appeals Chamber shall be the same as the term of office of the judges serving in the Appeals Chamber.

4. The members of the Appeals Chamber of the International Tribunal for the Former Yugoslavia shall also serve as the members of the Appeals Chamber of the International Tribunal for Rwanda.

5. After consultation with the permanent judges of the International Tribunal for Rwanda, the President shall assign such *ad litem* judges as may from time to time be appointed to serve in the International Tribunal for Rwanda to the Trial Chambers.

6. A judge shall serve only in the Chamber to which he or she was assigned.

7. The permanent judges of each Trial Chamber shall elect a Presiding Judge from amongst their number, who shall oversee the work of that Trial Chamber as a whole.

Article 14
Rules of Procedure and Evidence

The Judges of the International Tribunal for Rwanda shall adopt, for the purpose of proceedings before the International Tribunal for Rwanda, the Rules of Procedure and Evidence for the conduct of the pre-trial phase of the proceedings, trials and appeals, the admission of evidence, the protection of victims and witnesses and other appropriate matters of the International Tribunal for the former Yugoslavia with such changes as they deem necessary.

Article 15
The Prosecutor

1. The Prosecutor shall be responsible for the investigation and prosecution of persons responsible for serious violations of international humanitarian law committed in the territory of Rwanda

and Rwandan citizens responsible for such violations committed in the territory of neighboring States, between 1 January 1994 and 31 December 1994.

2. The Prosecutor shall act independently as a separate organ of the International Tribunal for Rwanda. He or she shall not seek or receive instructions from any government or from any other source.

3. The Office of the Prosecutor shall be composed of a Prosecutor and such other qualified staff as may be required.

4. The Prosecutor shall be appointed by the Security Council on nomination by the Secretary-General. He or she shall be of high moral character and possess the highest level of competence and experience in the conduct of investigations and prosecutions of criminal cases. The Prosecutor shall serve for a four-year term and be eligible for reappointment. The terms and conditions of service of the Prosecutor shall be those of an Under-Secretary-General of the United Nations.

5. The staff of the Office of the Prosecutor shall be appointed by the Secretary-General on the recommendation of the Prosecutor.

Article 16
The Registry

1. The Registry shall be responsible for the administration and servicing of the International Tribunal for Rwanda.

2. The Registry shall consist of a Registrar and such other staff as may be required.

3. The Registrar shall be appointed by the Secretary-General after consultation with the President of the International Tribunal for Rwanda. He or she shall serve for a four-year term and be eligible for re-appointment. The terms and conditions of service of the Registrar shall be those of an Assistant Secretary-General of the United Nations.

4. The Staff of the Registry shall be appointed by the Secretary-General on the recommendation of the Registrar.

Article 17
Investigation and Preparation of Indictment

1. The Prosecutor shall initiate investigations ex-officio or on the basis of information obtained from any source, particularly from governments, United Nations organs, intergovernmental and non-governmental organizations. The Prosecutor shall assess the information received or obtained and decide whether there is sufficient basis to proceed.

2. The Prosecutor shall have the power to question suspects, victims and witnesses, to collect evidence and to conduct on-site investigations. In carrying out these tasks, the Prosecutor may, as appropriate, seek the assistance of the State authorities concerned.

3. If questioned, the suspect shall be entitled to be assisted by Counsel of his or her own choice, including the right to have legal assistance assigned to the suspect without payment by him or her in any such case if he or she does not have sufficient means to pay for it, as well as necessary translation into and from a language he or she speaks and understands.

4. Upon a determination that a *prima facie* case exists, the Prosecutor shall prepare an indictment containing a concise statement of the facts and the crime or crimes with which the accused is charged under the Statute. The indictment shall be transmitted to a judge of the Trial Chamber.

Article 18
Review of the Indictment

1. The judge of the Trial Chamber to whom the indictment has been transmitted shall review it. If satisfied that a *prima facie* case has been established by the Prosecutor, he or she shall confirm the indictment. If not so satisfied, the indictment shall be dismissed.

2. Upon confirmation of an indictment, the judge may, at the request of the Prosecutor, issue such orders and warrants for the arrest, detention, surrender or transfer of persons, and any other orders as may be required for the conduct of the trial.

Article 19
Commencement and Conduct of Trial Proceedings

1. The Trial Chambers shall ensure that a trial is fair and expeditious and that proceedings are conducted in accordance with the Rules of Procedure and Evidence, with full respect for the rights of the accused and due regard for the protection of victims and witnesses.

2. A person against whom an indictment has been confirmed shall, pursuant to an order or an arrest warrant of the International Tribunal for Rwanda, be taken into custody, immediately informed of the charges against him or her and transferred to the International Tribunal for Rwanda.

3. The Trial Chamber shall read the indictment, satisfy itself that the rights of the accused are respected, confirm that the accused understands the indictment, and instruct the accused to enter a plea. The Trial Chamber shall then set the date for trial.

4. The hearings shall be public unless the Trial Chamber decides to close the proceedings in accordance with its Rules of Procedure and Evidence.

Article 20
Rights of the Accused

1. All persons shall be equal before the International Tribunal for Rwanda.

2. In the determination of charges against him or her, the accused shall be entitled to a fair and public hearing, subject to Article 21 of the Statute.

3. The accused shall be presumed innocent until proven guilty according to the provisions of the present Statute.

4. In the determination of any charge against the accused pursuant to the present Statute, the accused shall be entitled to the following minimum guarantees, in full equality:

(a) To be informed promptly and in detail in a language which he or she understands of the nature and cause of the charge against him or her;

(b) To have adequate time and facilities for the preparation of his or her defense and to communicate with counsel of his or her own choosing;

(c) To be tried without undue delay;

(d) To be tried in his or her presence, and to defend himself or herself in person or through legal assistance of his or her own choosing; to be informed, if he or she does not have legal assistance, of this right; and to have legal assistance assigned to him or her, in any case where the interest of justice so require, and without payment by him or her in any such case if he or she does not have sufficient means to pay for it;

(e) To examine, or have examined, the witnesses against him or her and to obtain the attendance and examination of witnesses on his or her behalf under the same conditions as witnesses against him or her;

(f) To have the free assistance of an interpreter if he or she cannot understand or speak the language used in the International Tribunal for Rwanda;

(g) Not to be compelled to testify against himself or herself or to confess guilt.

Article 21
Protection of Victims and Witnesses

The International Tribunal for Rwanda shall provide in its Rules of Procedure and Evidence for the protection of victims and witnesses. Such protection measures shall include, but shall not be limited to, the conduct of in camera proceedings and the protection of the victim's identity.

Article 22
Judgment

1. The Trial Chambers shall pronounce judgments and impose sentences and penalties on persons convicted of serious violations of international humanitarian law.

2. The judgment shall be rendered by a majority of the judges of the Trial Chamber, and shall be delivered by the Trial Chamber in public. It shall be accompanied by a reasoned opinion in writing, to which separate or dissenting opinions may be appended.

Article 23
Penalties

1. The penalty imposed by the Trial Chamber shall be limited to imprisonment. In determining the terms of imprisonment, the Trial Chambers shall have recourse to the general practice regarding prison sentences in the courts of Rwanda.

2. In imposing the sentences, the Trial Chambers should take into account such factors as the gravity of the offence and the individual circumstances of the convicted person.

3. In addition to imprisonment, the Trial Chambers may order the return of any property and proceeds acquired by criminal conduct, including by means of duress, to their rightful owners.

Article 24
Appellate Proceedings

1. The Appeals Chamber shall hear appeals from persons convicted by the Trial Chambers or from the Prosecutor on the following grounds:

   (a) An error on a question of law invalidating the decision; or

   (b) An error of fact which has occasioned a miscarriage of justice.

2. The Appeals Chamber may affirm, reverse or revise the decisions taken by the Trial Chambers.

Article 25
Review Proceedings

Where a new fact has been discovered which was not known at the time of the proceedings before the Trial Chambers or the Appeals Chamber and which could have been a decisive factor in reaching the decision, the convicted person or the Prosecutor may submit to the International Tribunal for Rwanda an application for review of the judgment.

Article 26
Enforcement of Sentences

Imprisonment shall be served in Rwanda or any of the States on a list of States which have indicated to the Security Council their willingness to accept convicted persons, as designated by the International Tribunal for Rwanda. Such imprisonment shall be in accordance with the applicable law of the State concerned, subject to the supervision of the International Tribunal for Rwanda.

Article 27
Pardon or Commutation of Sentences

If, pursuant to the applicable law of the State in which the convicted person is imprisoned, he or she is eligible for pardon or commutation of sentence, the State concerned shall notify the International Tribunal for Rwanda accordingly. There shall only be pardon or commutation of sentence if the President of the International Tribunal for Rwanda, in consultation with the judges, so decides on the basis of the interests of justice and the general principles of law.

Article 28
Cooperation and Judicial Assistance

1. States shall cooperate with the International Tribunal for Rwanda in the investigation and prosecution of persons accused of committing serious violations of international humanitarian law.

2. States shall comply without undue delay with any request for assistance or an order issued by a Trial Chamber, including but not limited to:

(a) The identification and location of persons;

(b) The taking of testimony and the production of evidence;

(c) The service of documents;

(d) The arrest or detention of persons;

(e) The surrender or the transfer of the accused to the International Tribunal for Rwanda.

Article 29
The Status, Privileges and Immunities
of the International Tribunal for Rwanda

1. The Convention on the Privileges and Immunities of the United Nations of 13 February 1946 shall apply to the International Tribunal for Rwanda, the judges, the Prosecutor and his or her staff, and the Registrar and his or her staff.

2. The judges, the Prosecutor and the Registrar shall enjoy the privileges and immunities, exemptions and facilities accorded to diplomatic envoys, in accordance with international law.

3. The staff of the Prosecutor and of the Registrar shall enjoy the privileges and immunities accorded to officials of the United Nations under Articles V and VII of the Convention referred to in paragraph 1 of this article.

4. Other persons, including the accused, required at the seat or meeting place of the International Tribunal for Rwanda shall be accorded such treatment as is necessary for the proper functioning of the International Tribunal for Rwanda.

Article 30
Expenses of the International Tribunal for Rwanda

The expenses of the International Tribunal for Rwanda shall be expenses of the Organization in accordance with Article 17 of the Charter of the United Nations.

Article 31
Working Languages

The working languages of the International Tribunal for Rwanda shall be English and French.

Article 32
Annual Report

The President of the International Tribunal for Rwanda shall submit an annual report of the International Tribunal for Rwanda to the Security Council and to the General Assembly.

BIBLIOGRAPHY

Abtan, Benjamin, ed. 2007. *Rwanda: Pour un dialogue des mémoires.* Paris: Albin Michel and Union des Etudiants Juifs de France.

Adelman, Howard. 2000. "Rwanda Revisited: In Search for Lessons." *Journal of Genocide Research* 2: 431–444.

Adelman, Howard and Astri Suhrke. 1996. *"Feilchen während Ruanda brennt." Der Überblick* 32: 7–11.

———, editors. 2000. *The Path of a Genocide: The Rwanda Crisis from Uganda to Zaire.* New Brunswick, NJ: Transaction.

Africa Confidential (1992–2003).

Africa Report (1992–1994).

African Union. 2000. *Rwanda: The Preventable Genocide.*

Berry, John A. and Carol Pott Berry, eds. 1999. *Genocide in Rwanda: A Collective Memory.* Washington, D.C.: Howard University Press.

Burkhalter, Holly J. 1994. "A Preventable Horror?" *Africa Report* 39: 17–21.

———. 1994/1995. "The Question of Genocide: The Clinton Administration and Rwanda." *World Policy Journal* 11: 44–54.

Carlsson, Ingvar, Han Sung-Joo, and Rufus M. Kupolati. 1999. *Report of the Independent Inquiry into the Actions of the United Nations during the 1994 Genocide in Rwanda.* New York: United Nations.

Chalk, Frank. 2000. "Hate Radio in Rwanda." In *The Path of a Genocide: The Rwanda Crisis from Uganda to Zaire,* edited by Howard Adelman and Astri Suhrke. 93–107. New Brunswick, NJ: Transaction.

Clapham, Christopher. 1998. "Rwanda: The Perils of Peacemaking." *Journal of Peace Research* 35: 193–210.

Clinton, William J. 1994. Remarks at the US Naval Academy Commencement Ceremony in Annapolis, Maryland. May 25.

———. 1994. "Executive Order 12918—Prohibiting Certain Transactions with Respect to Rwanda and Delegating Authority with Respect to Other United Nations Arms Embargoes." May 26. *Weekly Compilation of Presidential Documents* 30(21): 1171–1172.

Crampton, Ben. 2001. "Bringing Justice to Rwanda." *Times Literary Supplement,* August 10.

Dallaire, Roméo A. 1999. "The End of Innocence: Rwanda 1994." In *Hard Choices: Moral Dilemmas in Humanitarian Intervention,* edited by Jonathan Moore 71–86. Lanham, MD: Rowman & Littlefield.

Des Forges, Alison. 1995. "The Ideology of Genocide." *Issue: A Journal of Opinion* 23: 44–47.

Des Forges, Alison. 1999. *Leave None to Tell the Story: Genocide in Rwanda*. New York: Human Rights Watch.

Destexhe, Alain. 1995. *Rwanda and Genocide in the Twentieth Century*. New York: New York University Press.

Diop, Boubacar Boris. 2006. *Murambi: The Book of Bones*. Translated by Fiona Mc Laughlin. Bloomington, IN: Indiana University Press.

Fage, John Donnelly. 1978. *A History of Africa*. London: Hutchinson

Fromm, Erich. 1984. "Obedience as a Psychological and Moral Problem." In *On Disobedience and Other Essays*. 1–8. London: Routledge.

Grünfeld, Fred and Anke Huijboom. 2007. The failure to Prevent Genocide in Rwanda: The Role of Bystanders. Leiden: Brill.

Guichaoua, André. 1995. *Les crises politiques au Burundi et au Rwanda (1993–1994)*. Lille: Université des Sciences et Technologies.

Haag, Jan. 1997. "Rwanda." http://janhaag.com/POrwanda.html

Hintjens, Helen M. 1999. "Explaining the 1994 Genocide in Rwanda." *Journal of Modern African Studies* 37: 241–286.

Jaspers, Karl. 1948. *The Question of German Guilt*. Translated by E. B. Ashton New York: Doubleday.

Khadiagala, Gilbert M. 2002. "Implementing the Arusha Peace Agreement on Rwanda." In *Ending Civil Wars: The Implementation of Peace Agreements*, edited by Stephen John Stedman, Donald Rothchild and Elizabeth M. Cousens. 463–498. Boulder, CO: Lynne Rienner.

Klinghoffer, Arthur Jay. 1998. *The International Dimension of Genocide in Rwanda*. New York: Palgrave MacMillan.

Kuperman, Alan J. 2000. "Rwanda in Retrospect." *Foreign Affairs* 79: 94–118.

Lemarchand, René. 1995. "Rwanda: The Rationality of Genocide," *Issue: A Journal of Opinion* 23: 8–11.

———. 1996. *Burundi: Ethnic Conflict and Genocide*. New York: Woodrow Wilson Center and Cambridge University Press.

Magnarella, Paul J. 2000. *Justice in Africa: Rwanda's Genocide, Its Courts and the UN Criminal Tribunal*. Aldershot: Ashgate.

Mamdani, Mahmood. 1996. "Reconciliation without Justice," *Southern African Review of Books* 46: 3–5.

——— 2001. *When Victims Become Killers: Colonialism, Nativism and the Genocide in Rwanda*. Princeton, NJ: Princeton University Press.

Martin, Guy. 2002. "Readings of the Rwandan Genocide." *African Studies Review* 45(3): 17–29.

Mukagasana, Yolande. 1999. *N'aie pas peur de savoir—Rwanda: Une rescapée tutsi raconte*. Paris: Robert Laffont.

Ndorimana, Jean. 2001. *Rwanda 1994*. Rome: Vivere In.

Ngulinzira, Marie-Yolanda. 2001. "Hommage aux victimes de la tragédie rwandaise." In *Un autre Rwanda possible: Combat posthume, Boniface Ngulinzira*, by Florida Mukeshimana Ngulinzira. Collection Mémoires Africaines. 60. Paris: Harmattan.

Newbury, Catharine. 1988. *The Cohesion of Oppression: Clientship and Ethnicity in Rwanda, 1860–1960.* New York: Columbia University Press.

———. 1995. "Background to Genocide: Rwanda." *Issue: A Journal of Opinion* 23(2): 12–17.

Office of the High Commissioner. 2002 [1994]. *Statute of the International Tribunal of Rwanda.* United Nations. Human Rights.

Osbourne, Melissa. 2000. "Hutu Tutsi Rwanda Burundi." http://www.lyricalworks.com/poetry/hutututsi.htm

Pottier, Johan. 2002. *Re-imagining Rwanda: Conflict, Survival and Disinformation in the Late Twentieth Century.* Cambridge: Cambridge University Press.

Power, Samantha. 2001. "Bystanders to Genocide: Why the United States Let the Rwandan Tragedy Happen." *The Atlantic Monthly* 288: 84–108.

———. *"A Problem from Hell": America and the Age of Genocide* (New York: Basic Books, 2002).

Prunier, Gérard. 1999. "A Well Planned Genocide." *Times Literary Supplement*, October 22.

———. 1995. *The Rwanda Crisis: History of a Genocide.* London: Hurst.

———. 1996. "Der Westen könnte den Sumpf der Gewalt trockenlegen." *Der Überblick* 32: 4–6.

Quéméner, Jean-Marie and Eric Bouvet. 1999. *Femmes du Rwanda: Veuves du génocide.* Paris: Catleya.

Simpson, George Eaton and John Milton Yinger. 1985. *Racial and Cultural Minorities: An Analysis of Prejudice and Discrimination.* Fifth Edition. New York: Plenum.

Snedden, Doug. 1992. "Rwanda (Death Children)." http://www.dreamagic.com/cgi-bin/PoetryGen.cgi?author=Doug_Snedden&html=snedden&title=RWANDA_(death_children)&number=0001

Uvin, Peter. 1996. "Tragedy in Rwanda: The Political Ecology of Conflict." *Environment* 38: 6–15.

———. 1997. "Prejudice, Crisis, and Genocide in Rwanda." *African Studies Review* 40: 91–115.

———. 1998. *Aiding Violence: The Development Enterprise in Rwanda.* West Hartford, CT: Kumarian.

Vansina, Jan. 2004. Antecedents to Modern Rwanda: The Nyiginya Kingdom Madison: University of Wisconsin Press.

INDEX

www.ingramcontent.com/pod-product-compliance
Lightning Source LLC
Chambersburg PA
CBHW061016280326
41935CB00009B/994

* 9 7 8 1 7 8 1 7 9 5 8 0 4 *